THE MINDFUL COMMUNICATOR

by Nicholas Brice

"A superb book...a wake up call about what's important in life."
Sarah Hood
Global Head of Engagement
BUPA

THE **MINDFUL** COMMUNICATOR

by Nicholas Brice

To be like a tree
Planted by rivers of water
Bearing fruit in my season
My leaf will not wither
And everything I do will prosper.

...not like chaff that the wind just blows away.

COPYRIGHT AND DISCLAIMER

For permission requests, please contact:

Soul Corporations® Publishing
Visions Training & Development Limited (Reg No:2241851)
Maria House
35 Miller's Road
Brighton BN1 5NP
United Kingdom

Email: info@soulcorporations.com
Web: www.soulcorporations.com

ISBN: 978-1-7391053-0-3

Published by:

CONTENTS

DEDICATION

This book is dedicated to all the people who seek to make the world a better place. It is for those people who choose to use their talents and energies to increase joy, wellbeing, our quality of life, and to miminise suffering.

These are the true visionaries.

WHAT PEOPLE HAVE SAID ABOUT THIS BOOK

We desperately need to understand and meet the challenges of performing in the modern digital-hybrid working world; traditional approaches to developing leadership and followership are simply no longer appropriate. This book will help leaders and their teams embrace the behaviours and practices systemically that support diversity, equity and inclusion, make remote working really work, drive successful change, and create healthy, positive and meaningful work cultures that will attract and retain great people...and as a result, deliver top business performance from the inside out. We need new ideas for the new times we are living in. This much-needed book delivers them.

Dr Alan Beggs, Former Olympic Sports Psychologist, Director/Author at The Human Dimension Ltd

I really enjoyed it. I've always thought that if you can get just one good idea from a book it is worth reading...this one has lots of practical ideas you can use straight away by seeing the world through both an analogue and digital lens...happy reading!

John Neill, CBE, Chairman of Unipart Group of Companies

I think it's a superb book. I came at it thinking only of my professional life but was amazed at how the guidance and tools within it relate to our personal lives just as much as our working lives. In an increasingly complicated world rampant with negativity, its so easy to get sucked under, addicted to the things that help us escape or numb, like scrolling on phones, bingeing on box sets, shopping, food, drink...the list goes on and on.

This book is a wake up call about what's important in life. It's about being more present and more joyful in our day to day, with loads of exercises and tools to help us along the way. Really practical advice as well as thought provoking guidance and stories. It has inspired me to be more intentional about how I go about things.

Sarah Hood, Global Head of Engagement at Bupa

ACKNOWLEDGEMENTS

Dr Alan Beggs for his devotion to helping us get our ideas about business soul on paper and helping us ground our work in sound psychology.

Time Manager International (TMI) and Scandinavian Service School - in particular Claus Moller, Chris and Anthony Lane, Ann Beazer, Dr Janelle Barlow, Kostas Hatzigeorgiou, Jane Hunt, Peter Hancock, Chris Blumer, Sue Moore, Mike Pegg, Louise Jebson, Susanna Mitterer, Gillian James, Conor O'Connell and Sally-Ann Huson for their talents, positive challenge, inspiration, thought leadership and role modelling in creating a very special company with a purpose we're honoured to continue serving.

I want to include some stand-out clients who have inspired me in different ways over the years: Lord Colin Marshall at British Airways; Tomasso Zanzotto and Craig Dinsell at American Express; John Neill CBE at Unipart Group; John Howett and Chris Horée at Toyota-Lexus Europe; Erica McShane, Kim Baker and Aneliya Stoyanova at Progress. All of these great people have shown true leadership excellence in getting great results by inspiring and enabling people to be their best selves.

A big thanks also to Sarah Hood of BUPA and Abigail Barnes, Productivity Expert, and John Neill of Unipart for reviewing the content of the book. I would also like to thank Jasmine Fuego and Philip Kanaris from Zendesk for their insight and encouragement in its initial creation; Nick Rust, Katie Donaldson, Katie Hook and the rest of the the lovely team at Engage Business Media, plus Veronica Hannon and Daniel O'Connor at Transform Communications for their help with developing our new brands and getting this book out to all the people who can use it to create more joyful, soulful workplaces in our new digital world.

Book & Cover Design
Jennifer St John Loder, Studio11 Design
www.studio11design.co.uk

Proof Editing
Philip Reeve

PREFACE

The head of HRD came online from her office:

"I've heard from a colleague just how much you've been helping him in your coaching and what a good trainer you are. I have some sessions I'd love you to help us with."

She wanted some development sessions for her people. She was clear on what was needed:

"We spend much less time together than before COVID. We need to connect with each other. We need to find some meaningful ways to bring people together. Our people need to be able to speak confidently – to have impact and connect with others, and how to put a talk together too. And mindfulness – I know just how powerful this practice can be."

This was the brief. I thought about it. I did some research. I had studied neuroscience in business at MIT Sloan Management School the year before which had inspired me with some fresh ways of looking at some of my material, and I'd also been doing some research into the impacts of digital work on motivation and effectiveness. I started thinking:

"This can be my next book!"

I'd developed a lot of materials to coach senior executives in how to speak online and in person – including in a West End studio theatre with some groups from the Civil Service. My work builds on the TV and theatre direction work I've also been doing these past fifteen years. I had my twenty-five plus years on various conference stages helping clients change their culture successfully. I'd discovered that in both theatre and business blending mindfulness with performance skills can makes a big difference. Great, now I needed a title that was relevant to everyone in a business. Then it came to me in a flash:

THE MINDFUL COMMUNICATOR...

I also had some other great material to create an exciting new handbook for professional people working in a modern digital workplace. This would be a toolkit to help people connect with themselves and each other more effectively to meet our modern work-life challenges.

WHY THIS BOOK NOW?

We are living in a time of uncertainty and change in all aspects of life - environmental, social, political, economic and technological. Our minds are under constant distraction from these issues. Digital technology exacerbates this problem and now defines us in so many ways. With many of us working in hybrid work patterns, we are spending less time than ever in human company, and more time switched on and plugged in to smartphones and laptops/desktops.

Our attention is being pulled all over the place. How often do you find yourself reaching for a device or clicking on a link on your computer that takes you away from what is happening in the present moment, or reach out for your phone to check your apps or to check for new emails without even thinking?

Research in 2022 in the USA by Reviews.org[1] found people saying:
- 74% feel uneasy leaving their phone at home
- 71% check phones within the first 10 minutes of waking up
- 53% never go longer than 24 hours without their phone
- 64% use their phone on the toilet
- 61% have texted someone in the same room as them
- 48% feel a sense of panic or anxiety when their battery goes below 20%
- 45% say that their phone is their most valuable possession
- 43% use or look at their phone while on a date

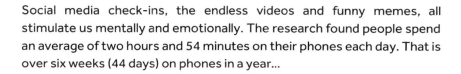

Social media check-ins, the endless videos and funny memes, all stimulate us mentally and emotionally. The research found people spend an average of two hours and 54 minutes on their phones each day. That is over six weeks (44 days) on phones in a year...

According to a University of California Irvine study[2], when distracted from a task or event, it can take us 23 minutes to return to full concentration. After only 20 minutes of regular interruption, people experience elevated stress, frustration, workload, effort, and pressure. Although we tend to complete tasks a little faster with the increased pressure, there is evidence we write less. So we may unconsciously abbreviate important communications and be less mindful of the needs of others. Working in this way may reduce the quality of our collective work climate over thousands and thousands of less mindful interactions.

Where do you stack up against these stats?

I think I want to change:

_____

_____

_____

If you want to make progress in these areas, this book may help you with some positive strategies to regain control.

I recommend a brilliant book: How to Break Up with Your Phone[3], in which Catherine Price describes how people who have grown up with smartphones are sometimes called the iGen (short for iGeneration). She quotes multiple studies that reveal the negative impact of the over-use of these kinds of technologies on our mental, emotional and even spiritual wellbeing. Add to this the impact of too many apps and icons on our computer screens, disorganised e-mail inboxes and poorly organized diary systems, we are in a potential mind-storm of digital distractions.

Gaining control

Being a mindful communicator is about managing yourself in the first instance: phone, laptop, social media, personal organisation, wellbeing practices, emotional intelligence etc., and then learning to manage others.

I'm sure you've met people who seem in control of what they are doing. They are like conductors of an orchestra - calm, controlled and wise, knowing what they need and where to find it, focusing on important relationships and building their support eco-systems. Whereas others are more like puppets being pulled around on several strings - restless, stressed out, distracted, ill-at-ease. Most of us vary between the two, depending on how life is going for us at the time.

In our journey, we'll help you introduce some simple methods and behavioural practices to become a more mindful communicator. We'll work on some ways to get more focused and to be able to connect with others and communicate important ideas to win their support.

What does 'being mindful' actually mean?

As human beings, we are a mix of capacities:

- Physical — using our senses and taking action
- Emotional — feelings about circumstances, relationships
- Mental — how we process information, strategize
- Spiritual — experiences that affect our spirit or soul

When we are being mindful, we are doing more than just using our minds. Our ability to think is very important of course, but when we are being mindful, we are more conscious of all four capacities in ourselves and other people. We are focused on the present moment, at the same time able to calmly acknowledge and accept how we and other people think and feel. You may also experience a deep spiritual quality - some call this soul - in your daily life, and share this experience with others.

For some, it also includes accessing a more spiritual dimension often achieved through practice: prayer, meditation, movement. For some, this experience only emerges at the sight of a beautiful sunset, or hearing inspiring music, or when going through profound experiences of some kind such as losing a loved one, falling in love, the birth of a child.

There is plenty of evidence to suggest that we can improve our lives by being fitter and more dextrous, being emotionally and intellectually intelligent, as well as having some kind of practice that keeps us connected with the deeper aspects of our existence.

A number of studies have reported the positive effects of meditation (see Wikipedia: Effects of meditation). The US Agency for Healthcare Research and Quality found that meditation practice can reduce psychological stress. Other studies show that mindfulness meditation can reduce symptoms of depression, improve mood, increase our resilience to stress and how well we can focus our attention. Other practices such as Yoga, T'ai chi, and meditation have been shown to have positive impacts on physical and psychological health.

UCB report that a 2014 study conducted by The Mind Health Report confirmed that people who engage in prayer for themselves and others as well as getting involved in a spiritual community are generally healthier and live longer. It seems like some kind of practice that suits your style is well worth establishing in your daily and weekly routines.

11

Mindful communicators

I'm sure you can think of some people – at work or home - you automatically want to engage with and listen to more than other people. What is it about them that inspires you to do this?

Who	Why I like communicating with them
Tereza	She has a calm authority She really listens to what I'm saying

And are there others who make you want to reach for your phone, or just move away and talk to someone else?

Who	Why I dislike communicating with them
Tony	He keeps interrupting Doesn't listen to me when I try to speak

When you look at the two types of person, what are the main differences? How many of the differences are aspects of how the person behaves that they could actually adjust if they were more mindful of how they communicate and the impact their behaviour has on you, as well as others?

Which group do you think you belong to? Most likely it will vary from person to person, as we often have a natural rapport with some people and less so with others. We are often naturally drawn to people we have things in common with. This is one of the challenges we all face in becoming truly inclusive and valuing diversity. Our minds like to use simplistic labels to categorise people as a 'type' rather than a unique individual. It helps us try to predict behaviour - based on race, sex, age, religion, socio-economic status, type etc. Being a mindful communicator means being fully open to tune into each individual in their own right.

This book is about the personal you and the professional you, who most likely needs to be able to win the support of a range of different people to achieve your goals.

It will help you focus on and practise life skills that are important outside our sometimes-mindless engagement with technology. It will give you new ways to communicate more deeply with yourself and with other people.

This book is aimed at helping you achieve three things:

1. Improve your professional impact when speaking: online or in-person
2. Create mutually supportive relationships with different people
3. Implement practices to reduce toxic stress and get more out of life

We've broken the booklet down into Seven Principles. Applying these principles may help you:

- Get more richness out of your experience of life at work and home
- Cultivate more satisfying professional and personal relationships
- Secure the support of key people who can help you achieve results
- Enhance your physical, mental and emotional wellbeing

Here are our Seven Principles:

1. Be fully present
2. Know who you are
3. Create the conditions
4. Be intentional
5. Organise your thoughts & communications
6. Cultivate mindful interactions
7. Create value for people

We started this introduction talking about trees.

As the old saying goes:

A good tree bears good fruit...
...a bad tree bears bad fruit.

Let's begin our journey by applying Principle 4: Be Intentional.

Success for me from this programme would look like:

1. _____
_____

2. _____
_____

3. _____
_____

14

PRINCIPLE 1
BE FULLY PRESENT

Be like a tree

Every time we take our attention away from what we are focusing on in the present moment, we are splintering our attention in different directions, reacting to what comes up with each email or message we focus our attention on.

Our habits can often mean we invite outside influences to over-stimulate our thoughts and feelings. It is a bit like eating too much food at a buffet - we can get sick, not necessarily physically, but with modern digital tech, there is growing evidence that nausea is mental and emotional. When we are in and out of digital systems, at best, we half-focus on important things and are tempted to skip from one thing to another.

At the end of the day, life is really a series of moments. We can influence the quality of these moments by our attitude, habits and behavioural choices. There is the potential for gold in most moments, but we may need to focus on creating them. It's a bit like the difference between panning for gold or swimming around in the dirt. Some people seem to live life from one positive moment to the next. Others spend much of the time restless and distracted, often feeling frustrated that their lives are not delivering what they want.

If we spend too much time focusing on past hurts, mistakes and resentments, and if we keep filling our heads with posts from people about what they did last weekend, we're reducing our connection with the present. And as we think of these things, our poor emotional system kicks in and we start to relive past upsets and pain.

We can also overthink the future as well as the past. Money worries, job insecurity, the presentation we have to give next week, the looming deadline for a major project we still haven't started working on—all these things can create what is sometimes called anticipatory anxiety.

Panning for gold or swimming in mud?

When we overthink the past and the future, metaphorically speaking, we are swimming around in the mud. When we learn to become fully present, we can change our attitude to pan for the gold in each moment: the smile of a young person, the way the light reflects off a window, a mundane but important task we need to do, the conversation we're having with a loved one, the thoughts we entertain, and those we detach from.

We're aiming at shifting our attention from:

PAST ··············· PRESENT MOMENT ··············· FUTURE

to...

PRESENT MOMENT

LEARNINGS FROM THE PAST ············· PRESENT MOMENT ············· INTENTIONS

The Deeper Self and Shallow Self

Living with real presence means deepening our awareness of what is happening right now. Dr. Alan Beggs worked personally as a psychologist with a number of Olympic Gold medallists at a time when TEAM GB's medal count increased to record levels. He talks about how the best performers had a 'glowing inner core' inside them in his super paper on Leading the Whole Person in the Digital Age[4]. This is all about the art of connecting to ourselves and others at the level of the Deeper Self.

Imagine you are looking out to sea and there is a storm blowing. The sea is churned up, tossing and frothing. Imagine a small boat being thrown around in the storm. If we were in this boat, we would be very anxious about what might happen. We may be cursing ourselves for not checking the forecast or for not having bought a different boat – because of past mistakes or even what others have done. We can so easily start adding the "blame game" to the stress of the situation.

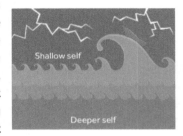

Shallow self

Deeper self

This is our experience when we are in our more surface level EGO mind. It is the more fragile, vulnerable sense of self that is too easily affected by life events, the opinions of others, our jealousies, and desires for personal significance.

This is the image of the "chaff that the wind blows away." With our relatively fragile, approval seeking, shallow ego in play, we are much more easily knocked off balance. We stand for nothing much and are not fully grounded in the present moment.

Things and people that take me away from my Deeper Self:

_____

_____

Shifting your focus: daily practice

If we shift our focus down into the depths of our ocean, things gradually become more still and unaffected. We can detach from concerns about the past or the future and settle into a calmer, more controlled and fully present state. This is the impact of mindfulness.

Here are some exercises you can use to become more fully present. They can be used in a daily practice and for preparing to make a presentation or to attend an important meeting. If you do these things, you will be much more grounded and focused and in a position to connect more deeply with others. You can also select one or more of these exercises to do for a minimum of 10-15 minutes a day to start with, once or twice a day. Try to build these exercises into your daily routine over time, and they will become life habits that will give you much greater control over your focus.

Research conducted in call centres[5] demonstrated that employees who spent 15 minutes at the end of the day reflecting about lessons learned performed 23% better after 10 days than those who did not reflect. A study of UK commuters found a similar result when those who were prompted to use their commute to think about and plan for their day. They were happier, more productive, and less burned-out than people who didn't.

17

EXERCISES
BE LIKE A TREE

Warm-Up & Becoming Present

Purpose: **To warm up and exercise your voice, body, presence, and your ability to connect with others.**

Outcome: **By connecting the voice, inner presence, movement, and connection with others, you will be able to communicate with others and speak in public with more confidence.**

So many presentation skills programmes try to get people to make all their gestures in a forced and conscious way. When you are fully present, your body will naturally move to support the ideas you are expressing. What you say and the way you say will be reflected your movements, which will often result in some natural gestures when they are needed. You can then save your use of conscious gestures for important illustrations: high-low, numbers in a sequence, wide or narrow focus etc.

How to do this exercise:

- Shake every part of your body to re-invigorate, to wake up, and to feel alive and present. Shake off the outside world and all worries. Put sound to shaking, maybe by humming or with an open mouth. Always make sure these exercises are done in a relaxed and natural way.
- Give yourself a face massage. Make sure your face is relaxed, with your jaw and tongue relaxed.
- Drop your chin, relax your tongue, throat, and tummy and breathe...
- Having shaken the body and massaged your face, come to stillness.

Exercises with thanks to Britt Forsberg[5]

In the Chinese martial art, Qigong, there is a technique called Zhan Zhuang. One of the most common Zhan Zhuang (pronounced "Jan Joo-ong") methods is known as Chēng Bào (this translates as the "tree hugging" stance...).

When you stand, you are like a tree.
You are growing from within.
Your feet, like roots, draw power from the earth.
Your body, like the trunk, is perfectly aligned.
You are unmoving, strong.
Your head is open to the heavens like the crown of the tree.
You rest calmly, the universe within your mind.
Master Lam Kam Chuen

It's a meditation designed to improve your connection with the present moment, your connection with your deeper self and the ability to connect more fully with people you speak to:

- Make sure the knees are in line with the hips. The knees are soft and bouncy, shoulders are soft, and back is straight, not slouching but not rigid. Wrists are soft.
- Imagine you are a puppet with a piece of string extending from your neck, through you head so you are relaxed, open, and alert.
- Come to stillness and look straight ahead.
- Allow your arms to extend slightly, as if you have placed them on either side of a tree trunk.
- Put all attention on your breathing. Where are you breathing from?
- Put attention to your diaphragm; this is where, as a communicator, all your energy and strength originates.
- Take a few natural deep breaths in and out; be aware that your diaphragm is expanding. You are lengthening and widening and not breathing from your chest.
- When breathing out, you may put some sound to it, in the form of a sigh to release any tension and to warm up the vocal cords.
- Repeat a couple times.
- Move one hand to your chest. Check that the chest isn't moving too much when breathing; shoulders and jaw should be relaxed.
- Take deep breaths rather than short sharp breaths.
- Breathe out with a big sigh (vocal) and collapse your lungs and 'DROP A LEVEL'. Allow the last bit of air out of your lungs and drop your awareness into your Deeper Self. Connect with your heart, your real self and the real purpose behind what you are about to say or do.

19

Becoming fully present

- Stand in the tree position. Feel your roots going down into the ground to give you stability.
- Breathe in the air that gives you life and energy and sigh out with feeling.
- Focus on the breath as it passes through your nostrils. Feel the air as it moves gently in... and out again. Feel the rhythm.
- If your mind wanders, don't worry, don't get frustrated. It's normal. Just gently guide it back to focus where you want it to. This is all good practice.
- Do this for three to five minutes.
- Let out a big sigh, feeling your emotions and drop a level as before. Collapse your lungs and become centered on your heart. "This is me. This is who I really am."
- Instead of connecting to all those thoughts, memories, and concerns about the past, the future, the presentation, the meeting, the day ahead...engage with your surroundings, one thing at a time... something you can see. Look, without judging. Look at an item for 5 seconds, for REAL, without judgement, then another, then another... for 2 minutes.
- Now listen to your surroundings without judging. Just listen to all the sounds – loud and quiet, near and far for 2 minutes.
- When you are ready, look at and engage with another person if you can – again, without judging. Have a chat. See how they are. Be present for them. Really see them, hear them. Listen with an open heart. Avoid any judging of yourself or them.
- If there are others, repeat. Keep listening fully to what they have to say. Listen for the feelings as well as the facts. Pay attention to them more deeply than when you are in Shallow Self mode.

Step outside for a while and calm your mind. It is better to hug a tree than to bang your head against a wall continually

Rasheed Ogunlaru

More ideas for your daily practice

My Right Book

- Spend time at the beginning of each day reviewing your intentions for the day (See Principle 4) and at the end of the day using a special notebook - your journal. Make a note of all the concrete ways you have been successful at the end of each day. This helps build and reinforce your thinking patterns as you grow.

Say 'Yes'

- Do some deep breathing exercises as before to become calm and centred.
- Think of something you have to do that you don't enjoy doing, or you feel too challenged by it, or even bored at the idea of having to do it. Understand that you may have simply programmed your brain to have this view. You may have been practising thinking this way every time the idea of doing it enters your mind.
- Now imagine this task is something you really want to do. Imagine doing the activity or the task joyfully and successfully. Picture the benefits you obtain from doing the activity or the task. Imagine yourself experiencing deep joy as you do it.
- Clench your fist as a signal to yourself to anchor this feeling. When you come to do it, you can clench your fist again to conjure the positive feelings again.
- Repeat for other tasks or activities.

Breaking patterns

- Spend 5-10 minutes doing your morning routines in a different way than you normally would. Take a shower instead of your normal bath. Brush your teeth with your left hand instead of the right. Eat a very different breakfast to normal – kippers perhaps? Take a different route to work than before.
- Focus fully on the present as you are doing this – savour it. What can you see, hear, feel that's different from normal. Practice presence.

Gratitude list

- Take a piece of paper and write down all the aspects of your life you are grateful for: health, family, friends, your home, your job, your talents, your colleagues, your potential for the future.
- Read back over each of these items and allow yourself to feel deeply grateful to have so many good things in your life today.

INTRODUCTION & PRINCIPLE 1

References and further reading

[1] www.reviews.org/mobile/cell-phone-addiction/
[2] www.ics.uci.edu/~gmark/chi08-mark.pdf
[3] How to Break Up With Your Phone: The 30-Day Plan to Take Back Your Life; Catherine Price; Trapeze (2019)
[4] Leading the Whole Person in the Digital Age; Dr Alan Beggs; 2022; Soul Corporations® www.soulcorporations.com/leading-the-whole-person-in-the-digital-age/
[5] Giada Di Stefano, Francesca Gino, Gary Pisano, and Bradley Staats; www.papers.ssrn.com/sol3/papers.cfm?abstract_id=2414478
[6] Exercises and concepts used with the permission of Britt Forsberg from her book: I Can't Do It! Why Did I Say Yes? Powerful Presence for Performers, Teachers and Public Speakers, Britt Forsberg, 2017.

For any thoughts or feelings...

_____

_____

_____

_____

_____

_____

_____

_____

_____

_____

_____

PRINCIPLE 2
KNOW WHO YOU ARE

Purpose and principles: my roots

We've talked about operating from the egoic, self-seeking Shallow Self and the richer, more conscious Deeper Self.

There are going to be times in life it when it gets windy.
An old Chinese proverb[1] says:

When the winds of change blow, some people build walls and others windmills

There are times in life when we might lose something or someone valuable to us. Unexpected challenges and crises at home and work might arise – family issues, health problems, financial worries, career loss/change. We may need to step into a role where we don't have the experience to be able to do it well from the outset. In these situations, we are often challenged to respond under pressure and sometimes in an emotionally-charged environment.

Intense pressure can seek out our weaknesses. It's easy to try to turn to quick-fix remedies to avoid dealing with the challenges we're facing.

Self-awareness is the key. Knowing who I am and what I stand for and being constantly aware of how I am feeling physically, emotionally and mentally is often 90% of the solution. Having these foundations and skills in place will mean I can adapt quickly to tricky situations without losing my balance. I am much less likely to be like 'the chaff that the wind blows away.'

Our Shallow Self is often more fragile than our Deeper Self. We are more likely to feel unsteady and restless in this state as we rely heavily on what the world can offer, or not. Remember our metaphor about the ocean. The deeper we go, the stiller we become and the more connected we feel to who we really are, as well as being more fully aware of other people and their deeper needs. We become more fully engaged with ourselves and each other.

23

The Deeper Self in business

Some people in business achieve success by detaching themselves from their own and others' feelings, and at worst, seeing other people, as well as the planet, as resources to be exploited in their pursuit of success.

Driven by a compelling desire to accumulate some kind of ego-significance as their first priority, they can find themselves disconnected from others. To some of these people, the idea of any kind of Deeper Self might even seem fluffy, irrelevant or quasi-spiritual.

This manifestation of the Shallow Self can result in an objectification of other people. We can all experience this at times. For example, have you ever experienced being late for an event when driving your car, or trying to get through a crowd quickly on a train station, and get annoyed by the 'irritating' people getting in your way? Let's face it, these are just people who have not left things as late as you have and are moving less hurriedly. And yet on another day, we may be relaxed and out on a drive or a day out, only for some 'idiot' in a hurry to tailgate us or push past to get ahead.

And if we become irritated, we can easily send subtle, and not-so-subtle messages of disapproval and judgement, which impact others and they may react in kind. Have you ever done this?

My former president at TMI, Claus Moller[2], told me a story to illustrate this point about a conversation at work in a busy office.

George is Alex's manager. There are a couple of key people off sick and the pressure is on to get things done. Alex and his wife both work, and he receives a call from their childminder that their son, Tom, has had a fall at school and has been rushed to hospital and is in Accident and Emergency. Alex's wife is away on a business trip.

Alex approaches George:

Alex: Hi George, I'm so sorry, one of my kids has had a fall at school and is in hospital. I really need to see them. My partner is away on a business trip.

George: (looking at his watch and sighing with a touch of exasperation) Ahh... Alex. Yes, our policy is to allow people time for this kind of thing. You can go. But as we are so busy, I expect you back today if it's not serious.

How personally motivated do you think Alex feels to get back to work to help out after this response from George? How much consideration is George showing for what Alex is dealing with?

Have you ever found yourself in a situation where other peoples' needs seem to be in conflict with yours, rather than seeing them as having needs and wants just like you have? When we live too much in a world of facts, the Shallow Self can see others as potential barriers to us getting our needs met.

How about if George was a manager who responded this way:

Alex: Hi George, I'm so sorry, one of my kids has had a fall at school and is in hospital. I really need to see them. My partner is away on a business trip.

George: Oh Alex, I am sorry. Is it little Tom or Mary?

Alex: It's Mary. Second time this term.

George: Yes, I remember. Of course, you must get down there. Please do take a taxi on the company if that helps. Please let me know how you are both getting on when you get a chance. I am concerned.

In this second example, George fully acknowledges the significance of this situation and Alex's deeper needs as a fellow person - not just a human resource. He is a leader who puts people first. He may still be highly results-focused but he gets things done with a deeper level of engagement from the people around him. As he is leading from his Deeper Self, he reads the situation in both a bottom-line way as well as a beyond-the-bottom-line way, as Claus used to say. So, in conclusion, let's look at the differences between these two worlds:

Bottom-Line World	Beyond-the-Bottom-Line World
People are resources	People are body-mind-heart-soul
Planet is a source of resources	Planet is a living eco-system
Facts come first	Facts and feelings come first
Success from people	Success through people
Driven by shallow ego-mind	Driven by deeper principles (roots)

In the modern business world, to achieve sustained success, we must inspire the best from other people: their passion, integrity, honest endeavour, dynamic energy, and willingness to co-operate with others
Dr Alan Beggs

The sources of wisdom

When we become practitioners of a more grounded way of living from the Deeper Self, we can focus our attention on developing more wisdom, knowledge and understanding as we move through life. I enjoy reading some wise words from various sources as part of my daily practice each morning. King Solomon[3] was known for his wisdom. Some of the wise sayings we use in our modern world were created by him:

Pride goes before destruction, a haughty spirit before a fall.

Your soul is nourished when you are kind; it is destroyed when you are cruel.

All problems are people problems. And most people problems are people refusing to act like people.

One who masters their passions is better than a conqueror of a city.

I also find inspiration in the work of Islamic philosopher Rumi[4]:

If you are irritated by every rub, how will your mirror be polished?
When you do things from your soul, you feel a river moving in you, a joy.

There are other Arabic proverbs[5] that are very insightful:

Be in the world, but not of the world.
A change is as good as a rest.
A little spark can kindle a great fire.

حكمة

...and Chinese proverbs such as these from Lao Tzu[6]:

The journey of a thousand miles begins with a single step.

If you are depressed you are living in the past.
If you are anxious you are living in the future.
If you are at peace you are living in the present.

26

What is wisdom?

Wisdom is about finding ways to understand what is happening in our lives and how to make good choices. It is about becoming open to insights and understanding that come from outside of ourselves. In life, there are no real certainties. But wisdom is about being inspired by ideas and principles that are probably going to improve our chances of a better quality of life - or by not following them, things will probably not work out too well!

The word 'inspiration' literally means:

- Being stimulated to do or feel something, especially to do something creative: "I had a flash of inspiration."
- Being inspired by a person, event or happening: "she was an inspiration to the entire team."
- It can also mean the drawing in of your breath; inhaling air.

So, to gain wisdom, we may need be open to inspiration from a source outside of our own self: an idea that can come to us from somewhere; a person we meet says something that triggers an idea; we are in a period of deep reflection, possibly even asleep, and an idea appears like magic - from somewhere - that solves an important problem we've been wrestling with.

When you invest time in daily practice, you are looking to create a window of opportunity to open up your Deeper Self to access insights and wisdom about the choices you need to make in life.

To revisit our tree metaphor, we need to remain open within ourselves to draw in oxygen, water and important nutrients to grow and develop. But if we become too caught up in our own world and live in the turbulent, isolated, busy world of the Shallow Self, we may lose our ability to receive wisdom from higher sources of intelligence. In some spiritual texts, heaven and earth are described as being to do with our real experiences of life here on earth.

Clarify your personal values

Research conducted by James Kouzes and Barry Posner[7] shows that people who have clear personal values are more committed in their daily activities at work than people who don't - irrespective of the values of the organization. When you become fully grounded in your personal purpose and principles, you will find it much easier to live through your authentic self - and keep centred when the going gets tough.

When the sun is shining and everything is going well, it's easy to find life to be a rich and positive experience. But when things are not going so great, we can live a deeper and more rewarding life by focussing on the fruits we are creating in our own life and in others' lives (see Principle 7).
We can choose to focus on creating fruit that lives on in memories. This fruit lives so much longer than the temporary fix of a social media exchange, some cool memes, spending money, or eating and drinking too much.

When we are fully grounded in the Deep Self, we're less inclined to need gratification through things that just appeal to our senses and the never-satisfied, egoic identity, such as food, sex, money, and prestige. It's this part of us that is tempted by the promises of cool marketing campaigns, and we get sucked more easily into seeking pleasure. As we've seen, when the rain comes and the wind starts blowing, if we are only driven by these pleasures, we are easy targets for getting knocked off balance.

When we live shallow lives, we can find ourselves and the choices we make being driven by the qualities of the shallower ego:

Anger: Lashing out at ourselves or others who rub us up the wrong way.

Pride: Exaggerated sense of self-importance - a distortion of our ego.

Vanity: Admiring our own appearance or achievements far too much.

Gluttony: Consuming food and other resources wastefully.

Greed: Being driven to possess more than we need - wealth, power, food...

Lust: Extreme passion/longing for sex, money, power, prestige.

Envy: Resenting others for what they have and their quality of life.

Laziness: Avoiding chores we don't enjoy or find challenging.

If we know who we are and what we stand for, and if we know the real results we are looking to achieve in life, we can be like the tree that is firmly rooted, that bends when the wind blows without breaking. We are better equipped to respond to challenges without breaking or being blown away. And when the trouble passes, we are less likely to have let ourselves or others down. We retain a sense of our deeper identity. We are less likely to have reacted in ways that undermine our sense of value – or if we have made mistakes, then we are strong enough to clean things up with the people affected quickly and authentically and restore the balance in our lives. We acknowledge mistakes authentically and seek to make amends in good time, rather than let relationships deteriorate to the point they can't be recovered.

If we don't keep clearing the debris from the mistakes we make, we gradually build up baggage that can weigh heavily over time. We may even try to blame other people or situations for the bad choices we make. Sure, other people, in their own weakness and vulnerability, may do things that cause us to fall out of balance.

Clumsy people - staying grounded

Many people are heavily focused on themselves and can be clumsy - with themselves and others. They may be driven by the needs of their own ego. But if we react in kind, in ways that don't reflect our deeper principles and sense of purpose, we just collaborate in building up the baggage. Instead of digging for gold, we all end up swimming in the mud.

We trade warm, positive relationships with frosty exchanges, and often we start to find fault.

Too much snow and ice often breaks even the strongest tree if it's allowed to build up. When we lose the rich connection with our Deeper Self, we often seek all sorts of gratification to replace this important sense of self-worth, and the process continues.

Case study: The Presentation

Imagine you have been asked to do a presentation in the next few days on a topic you have never presented about before. Perhaps someone sends you a set of visual aids to use that you are unfamiliar with. The slides are poorly designed, full of formatting errors, and far too busy to be effective as visual aids. Making a good presentation will take some concentrated effort, but you have other challenges going on.

You have choices:

1. You push back, saying you don't know the subject well enough and don't have enough time to prepare.

2. You stumble through the slides you are sent, making sure the audience is reminded that you didn't design them and it's not your material.

3. You commit to doing your best with this presentation, taking some time to make the slides your own. You create a clear contract with your audience at the beginning of the presentation and what you will cover. You promise to look into answers for any questions you can't answer.

Which option would you most likely go for: 1), 2) or 3)?

I would suggest that 1) and 2) represent someone operating out of their egoic shallow self. They are reactive responses that seek self-preservation as the priority. And by seeking it, we actually risk causing more damage to our sense of self-worth. When we see things through the eyes of our Deeper Self, we can see the potential for making the best contribution we can in most situations. We may see it as difficult, yes, but it is an opportunity to learn and to grow as well. We do our best to create some gold for ourselves and others that will remain in our story forever.

At a pinch, opting for a combination of 1) and 3) is at least better than just doing a poor job and blaming the lack of preparation time you had:

"I am already feeling over-committed on some important priorities. I'm happy to help, so can we look at some other ways to cover this? I am happy to give input with the design if we can find another person who will do the actual presentation."

But most importantly, which strategy will reveal the most permanent sense of personal satisfaction?

If we are rooted in who we are and what we are doing in the present moment, we can look for the gold in every situation. We may experience stress, but a certain amount of stress is part being alive and growing to our potential. The better we can become at being fully present whilst knowing that we are feeling under pressure, the more likely we are to be able to adopt some strategies to deal with it. It would go like this:

1. **Awareness: What is happening in my mind, body, emotions?**
I've been asked to do this presentation with little notice. The slides are really poor. I don't know much about this subject, and I have three days to prepare. I'm feeling challenged and scared. My breathing rate is shallow and quick. My mind is racing. I am experiencing self-doubt. I feel sick. I want to blame someone.

2. **Take a pause: Breathe deeply**
I can't trust my first response, as my egoic Shallow Self is driving me. I've learnt that the stress response is a primal reaction from the days when we were cavemen faced with predators – we either fight, freeze or flee. I'm experiencing all three right now. I need to go somewhere to breathe and focus. I'll pop into the stress management cubicle out by the lift. I've done some of my best thinking there. I can do some mindfulness breathing exercises and refocus on my objective.

3. **Explore my choices and the consequences of each**
What's the real result I want to achieve? This presentation is about improving my team's performance, and I do care about this. I also want to improve my presentation skills. I can offer to do my best with this presentation, taking some time to make the slides my own. I have time to do a little research. I will learn something here, although I do feel very challenged by it, but challenges result in learning and growth. Feeling challenged is a good thing. I will look for the gold in this opportunity, rather than swim around in the mud. Ralph did that last week with the budgeting project. It wasn't pretty, but I'm pleased I helped him out. This is the real me.

4. **Refocus and choose the right action**
I will make this presentation my own and do my best. I can easily manage audience expectations at the beginning of the presentation and what I will be able to cover and what I won't. I can take questions and if I can't answer, I can note the question and offer to get back to people, or there may be people in the audience who can comment.

31

EXERCISE

MY BEST SELF STORY

Think of a time in your life when you would say, "This was me at my best." It can be in a work situation or in your home life. It can be something you did on your own or with others. The key is to pick a story that is true and represents you at your very best:

When I...

_____

_____

_____

How did this experience impact you physically, mentally, emotionally, spiritually?

_____

_____

_____

Now repeat the process for an experience when you were Your Worst Self. What do the differences teach you about you?

Clarifying my purpose and principles

Your values are the deeper, soul-level principles that are the basis for your personal DNA. They are the roots of what define you as a person and as a professional.

Your true values often represent the beliefs you've developed over a lifetime of experiences about how you feel you should live your life. Your audience will also have their own, as we've explored earlier, and the Mindful Communicator takes steps to connect with these.

32

Knowing our beliefs and those of our audience is key to getting results. Our values and beliefs determine our attitude and behaviour. Of course, the choices we make about our actions are the result of the beliefs (and values) we have, which have been formed over years of experiences and memories we have collected.

You may know and be clear on your own personal sense of purpose and principles - your root system. If you aren't, that doesn't mean you don't have any; it just means they aren't yet clear to you. When you act in harmony with your Deeper Self, then you are most likely to feel good about yourself and proud of your behaviour. When you don't live by them, you may feel unhappy, that something is missing in your life; possibly, you may even look for someone to blame. Your surface level, ego-mind will take over and look for more distractions through gratification of some kind, as we explored earlier.

You may work in an organisation whose values resonate with yours, and you may not. If not, then you will be spending a lot of energy trying to fit in.

We have life values and professional/work values. Here we want to think about the professional beliefs, principles, and values that lie at the heart of our work. When we seek to understand and appreciate others too, we can take concrete steps to bring some real depth and impact to all our communications.

Values are like footprints. Nobody's are the same, but you leave them all over everything you do.
Elvis Presley

EXERCISE
MY PURPOSE AND PRINCIPLES

Use the following examples and circle some key words that resonate especially deeply with you. This can help you identify the core principles or values that underpin your life at work and at home.

Examples:

- *I am truthful, sincere, and frank; honesty is the best policy for me.*

- *I act in a moral and ethical way, doing what I say I will do.*

- *I believe in being free from bias/injustice and in being even-handed.*

Reliability Loyalty Commitment Open-mindedness Honesty Efficiency Innovation Creativity Autonomy God Fun Adventure Individuality Positivity Inspiring Passion Respect Giving Wellbeing Courage Sustainability Respect Love Nurturing Service Integrity Truthfulness Family Contribution Creativity Teamwork Charity Fitness Equality

Additional words important to you:

_____

Identify the 3-4 most important beliefs and values you hold about how you should act and behave in your professional life. Your roots:

I ...

_____

_____

I...

_____

_____

I...

_____

_____

Your core purpose is the reason you do your best when you do your best. When we are living in harmony with this purpose, we're often almost unaware of time passing. Without effort, we're fully absorbed in what we're doing and we are naturally full of energy and commitment.

How would you define your core purpose in your work today? You may choose to do the same for your life in general, at home as well as at work.

In a nutshell, I believe my purpose is to:

_____

_____

_____

Having clarity about these things can help anchor you in your root system and find strength in being your true self rather than trying to be someone you think will win the approval of others – or being "the chaff that blows away."

It is important to be able to simply summarise answers to the following questions in any situation:

Why am I here today? What are the real results I am aiming to achieve?

_____

_____

_____

_____

How will I measure success? What will be happening when I succeed?

_____

_____

_____

_____

PRINCIPLE 2
References and further reading

[1] www.wealthygorilla.com/79-chinese-proverbs/
[2] www.clausmoller.com/en/books/
[3] www.biblestudyministry.com/proverbs-solomon-daily-wisdom/
[4] www.leverageedu.com/blog/rumi-quotes/
[5] www.leslistes.net/top-101-arabic-proverbs/
[6] www.goodreads.com/author/quotes/2622245.Lao_Tzu
[7] The Leadership Challenge: How to Make Extraordinary Things Happen in Organizations (J-B Leadership Challenge: Kouzes/Posner); Jossey-Bass; 6th edition (13 Jun. 2017) See https://www.leadershipchallenge.com

For any thoughts or feelings...

_____

_____

_____

_____

_____

_____

_____

_____

_____

_____

PRINCIPLE 3
CREATE THE CONDITIONS

What is the good soil: conditions I need to grow?
What is bad soil: the conditions that hamper me?

No matter how good a seed is, if it is planted in poor soil or overly dry conditions, it will rarely grow much, if at all.

As human beings, we have a remarkable capacity to grow and develop in many different directions. The better the conditions we create for ourselves and each other, the healthier and more vibrant we will become.

Think back to the My Best Self exercise you did in Principle Two.

When you did the exercise, what were some of the conditions that helped you achieve what you managed to achieve? Who else was involved? How can you focus on creating more soil with more nutritious conditions to help you achieve more in life?

Maintaining optimal performance

During my studies of neuroscience with MIT Sloan Management School[1] , Dr. Tara Swart asked us to read her book, The Source[2]. She explains in it how the quality of our overall functioning is related to our lifestyle practices, which in turn affects the quality of our thinking and how we see and interact with the world we find ourselves in.

In her book she shows how research has identified that our work patterns and lifestyle habits can also have a potent impact on our higher cognitive functioning.

I recommend her book and the MIT programme for further study.

The quality of our brain health profoundly affects our abilities to do the following:

- Learning
- Thinking
- Reasoning
- Remembering things
- Solving problems
- Making quality decisions
- Concentration
- Paying attention, sharp focus

Look after our brains

The quality of our overall brain functioning is related to our lifestyle practices. In her brilliant book, Dr. Swart recommends we focus on developing good habits around the following:

- Rest
- Fuel
- Hydration
- Oxygenation
- Personal organisation

We need our rest

The science suggests that sleeping less than 7 hours a night is not healthy or sustainable for 98–99% of the population. Apparently our brain's glymphatic cleansing system takes 7–8 hours to flush out toxins, which can otherwise build up to form the pathology of dementia-type diseases.

I try to commit to 7 to 9 hours of sleep per night, with 8 as an average, and a reasonably regular sleep routine. I've found through experience that I need to avoid digital devices or TV screens for at least an hour before I go to sleep too. If I am working hard on projects, I also find meditation in the evening in addition to the morning also helps me switch off.

Pay attention to what we put in the tank

According to research (Drubach[4]) your brain is 2% of your bodyweight, but it takes up at least 20% of the body's energy. Therefore, we are advised to eat a nutritious diet richly populated with vegetables and fruit, whole grains, good fats from olive oil, avocados, and oily fish, and to reduce our intake of sugar and processed food.

Drink up!

According to USGS[5], an adult male needs about 3 litres of water per day while an adult female needs about 2.2 litres per day. Some of this water is contained in the food we eat. Carrying water with you at all times and sipping regularly is a very good idea if you are looking for optimal brain functioning.

I sometimes swap some of my caffeinated drinks for herbal tea and it goes without saying how much evidence there is to support the limiting of alcohol and sugary drinks.

Exercise regularly: oxygenate

Pick a form of exercise that you enjoy and schedule regular, varied-pace workouts to help raise your oxygen level and activate all your muscle groups. Much of the guidance I have unearthed suggest you need to exercise for around 20-30 minutes, three times a week, so that you are out of breath and perspiring (please check with a doctor first).

Get organised!

Is your home calm and happy? Are you overloading your attention by using very cluttered workspaces and surroundings - physical and digital? This may be draining your mental resources. It's a good idea to focus on periodically clearing, filing, ordering, and stripping away clutter as much as you can.

Do you work in an area where you can think clearly? Are you overloading your brain with stimulation and rewards from digital devices? Most apps are designed to try to entrap your attention for long periods. Do you live and work in untidy, disorganised conditions? We can easily create a feeling of overload if we can't see our challenges and priorities clearly. Being structured in how we approach things can help (see Principle Five).

_____

_____

_____

_____

_____

_____

Nourishing your soil

Have you noticed that when you are in the presence of some people, you feel more energised and confident than when you are with others?

We all need energy and vitality to be our best selves. In his lovely book The Hidden Life of Trees[6], Peter Wohlleben quotes scientists in the Harz Mountains in Germany who have discovered that individual trees of the same species are often connected to each other through their root systems. They exchange nutrients and help each other when needed, as by chance their roots find each other under the soil as they grow. They create an eco-system by collaborating with each other.

We can elect to connect with each other at the root level. We can find similarities of spirit, although we may have different strengths. We can be nutritious allies or toxic rivals.

There are people who can nourish your soil and there are people who will poison it! A warm response, kind words, an offer to help out, empathy with our point of view, some gratitude for something we have done, or certain activities can all help give us energy.

Criticism, spite, ridicule, or being ignored, dismissed, or marginalised can make us feel cast down. Being isolated without any recognition can quickly cause a deterioration of psychological wellbeing. Research[8] has linked social isolation and loneliness to the risk of mental health issues like depression, anxiety, cognitive decline, Alzheimer's disease and substance abuse, as well as chronic conditions like high blood pressure, heart disease, obesity, and diabetes.

People who are more socially connected have been shown to have less inflammation in the body; on the contrary, those who are more isolated and lonely show increased chronic inflammation.

Who are the people in your network who may be suffering from isolation and lack of connection? What can you do about it? How can you reach out to them and make then feel part of something?

Given our modern, hybrid, home-working climate, the research also found that the effects of social isolation become worse when people are placed in physically isolated environments.

Certain activities or tasks may be so far from our strengths and motivations that we soon run low on energy. Sometimes it's our own attitude to what we're doing that drains us, and that of others, as we complain and gripe about "having" to do a particular thing.

When we're swimming in the mud and not mining for gold, we often feel tired and listless from the effort.

41

Soil fillers

How rich is your soil? How confident are you in your ability to handle challenges with grit and energy? Who are the people and what are the activities that give you energy? How can you spend more time in these situations and with these people?

_____

_____

_____

_____

_____

_____

Knowing your strengths and making sure you spend time using those strengths will add to your energy. Don't forget, some people are extroverts; they gain energy from company and lose it from being alone too much. Others are more introverted and need time alone to recharge. These people often find being with others, particularly loud and demanding people, an ordeal after a short period of time.

What are your strengths? When do you come alive?
When does time pass without you noticing?

_____

_____

_____

_____

_____

_____

_____

How can you do more of these things?

_____

_____

_____

_____

Soil killers

We can easily create toxicity in our lives by spending time with people and in places that drain our energy. The way we organize ourselves at work and home can also be problematic.

Addictive overuse of digital devices is known to likely damage our mental and emotional wellbeing. Healthsite[7] report ten possible health hazards from overusing phones including cancer, sleep disorders, increased accident risk and even heart problems.

There may well be some tasks and activities that need doing where you turn into a soil killer for yourself and others with your attitude. When I was a kid, cleaning my room, eating root vegetables, and "having" to walk the dog were all enough to bring in the thunder clouds.

Who are the people and what are the things you do that cost you energy and vitality? How can you reduce their impact?

_____

_____

_____

_____

How to manage stress*

What do you mean when you say, "I feel stressed"?

Have you experienced periods in life when you have felt depressed, tense, angry, low, or tired all the time... or a combination of all of these?

The thing is, pressure can equate to higher performance. If we did not experience pressure, we would most likely not be alive. Our stress response is the reaction we have as humans to intense situations where it's life or death. Cast your mind back a few thousand years...

Going down the road (if there was one) would most likely be much more challenging than today. We might meet a raptor or sabre tooth tiger and if we did we would get a sudden, massive, physical burst of energy. This would give us super strength within a split second and we would most likely do one of two things:

 Try to hit the animal with our best shot
OR
Run like crazy up the nearest tree

...or rather like the rabbit in the headlights, it might all be too much, and we would stand very still while the animal likely devoured us.

Physically, we would experience some of the following immediate reactions. All of these are about us achieving peak performance in less than a second:

• **Fast, shallow breathing**	*to get lots of oxygen into our blood stream*
• **Massive production of adrenalin**	*the hormonal "go switch" (and a good painkiller)*
• **Rise in heart rate and blood pressure**	*circulate oxygenated blood to the muscles*
• **Faster clotting of the blood**	*useful with smaller injuries*
• **Faster metabolism**	*turning our fat into energy*
• **Reduction of blood in the stomach**	*our muscles need the oxygen more*
• **Reduction of tension in the bowels**	*maybe to try to put the animal off eating us*
• **Sharper senses**	*see the best way to escape*

*With special thanks to Dr Janelle Barlow for her permission to include material adapted from her books on Stress Management in this publication.

All these responses are great for:

- Getting our minds working at top speed
- Seeing options much faster, as if time were slowing down
- Sharper attention and focus
- Improvement of short-term judgement

The key point here is that all these reactions are great for a short-term challenge. When we are facing an important challenge, such as making a presentation, we can use this energy to increase our presence online or in a room, but we can't maintain this over a long period, especially if there are other stressors in our lives that we are not handling so well.

But our stress can be the accumulation of lots of stressors over a longer period. This is when we experience toxic stress, which is often self-reinforcing as we create ever more stress for ourselves and each other by responding in ways that cause a deterioration in all areas of our wellbeing: physical, mental, emotional, and ultimately spiritual. Too much poorly managed change, poor working conditions, relationship issues, and money worries can all add up to a long-term stress problem if we don't have skills to tackle these things in a calm and controlled way.

Negative stress

Stress becomes toxic when it's a long-term reaction to an overload of an accumulation of poorly handled stressors over a period of time. It may not be one thing that causes the deterioration in our physical, mental, emotional, and spiritual wellbeing. It's often a combination of factors and how we experience overload.

Let's introduce a model here to define the process by which we deal with pressure. Positive impacts are inspired performance, energy, grit, and tenacity. These responses can create a reduction in the impact of the stressors we face.

This can create a virtuous circle as we respond positively to even very challenging situations, and each time, we grow a bit more.

It can also become a vicious circle when our stress responses create negative impacts, and we create more stress for ourselves and others.

My pressure management plan

You can always improve your skills in handling stress, becoming more resilient and capable of handling greater and greater challenges.

We have two options to turn a vicious cycle into a virtuous cycle:

1. Increase our skills to respond positively to stressors.
2. Increase our skills and habits to manage our stress response.

Here is a step-by-step process you can use to create a plan to achieve this:

Step One: Spot your stress signals

Put a mark against the ones you recognise when you are experiencing too much stress. Examples of reactions to toxic stress include:

Physical

- Change in breathing rhythm
- Tense, aching muscles
- Headaches
- Sweating
- Cold hands and feet
- Changes in appetite
- Stomach problems, heartburn, hiccups

Mental

- Lack of concentration
- Mistakes
- Forgetful/absent-minded
- Over-reaction
- Poor judgement

Emotional

- Irritability/short temper
- Nervousness
- Depression/silence
- Emotional outbursts, crying
- Talking too much or too loudly

Behaviour

- Insomnia
- Increased eating and drinking
- Absenteeism
- Clumsiness

Spiritual

- Lack of purpose - meaning
- Coldness
- Lack of hope
- Cynicism
- Addictive "fixing" patterns: sex, drugs, alcohol, money, power, prestige, possessions, control, self-obsession
- Restlessness
- Dissatisfaction

Step Two: Identify your stressors

Below is a list of common stressors.
See which of these you recognise.
Perhaps put a mark against ones that affect you.

Sources of stress can include:

• **Physical**	*Too cold/hot, noise, illness, working conditions, overeating/drinking*
• **Mental**	*Lack of organisation, overload from digital devices, deadlines*
• **Emotional**	*Loss of loved ones, relationship breakdowns, revisiting past hurts*
• **Social**	*Demanding co-workers/manager, family, jealousy, conflict*
• **Economic**	*Money problems, debt, bills, inflation, tax, rent/mortgage*
• **Technology**	*Poorly designed systems, equipment breakdowns, lack of skill/training*
• **Culture**	*Different values/political views, uncertainty/change*

We can't possibly know all the factors at play in a colleague or family member's world. It's therefore easy to misread the effects of toxic stress as lack of motivation or willingness when a person appears listless and lacking in enthusiasm. And if we misread this and put the person under more pressure to "pull themselves together," then we may become the straw that breaks the camel's back. We can potentially damage their health, rather than be the supportive ally they need more than anything during such a tough period.

Who do I know who might be experiencing toxic levels of stress?

_____

_____

Step Three: Keep a daily journal

Changing our habitual responses may mean we need to make some sub-conscious reactions more conscious. A great way to do this is to spend 10 minutes each morning writing down how you are feeling about all the things you are experiencing in life, and how you are responding. Emptying our thoughts and feelings on paper can often help relieve tension. We can also add entries before we go to bed, marking down all the examples of progress we have made that day. When we spend some "me-time" like this, we can spot patterns of reaction and learn about how we can change the role we are playing in the situations we are facing.

Step Four: Analyse and treat your stressors

Keeping focused on the life events you are experiencing and the way you are reacting will give you a much better window to practice consciously adapting your reactions, and most importantly, knowing when you need to make amends to other people if you have behaved poorly in a situation, before their resentments fester and harden their attitude towards you. It's far better to clear debris on a daily basis to keep the water clean for feeding our trees and those of others.
Regular journaling can really help with this process.

You have four options with each stressor:

1. **Take action:**
Can we learn new skills, get some information, and turn it into one of our goals? For example, if you have to make a presentation, you can get some training, practice and set an intention to learn from the experience, and do it as well as you can.

2. **Get away:**
Sometimes, we can just avoid exposure to the stressor(s). If someone is being confrontational or just plain difficult, you can get some altitude mentally and tell yourself you are on the receiving end of someone else's ineffective stress response.

3. **Do nothing:**
There are times when no action is possible. You must sit it out and just wait, e.g., when you are waiting for an organisation announcement on budgets that will affect your role, or when you are waiting for the results of medical tests.

4. **Reframe your attitude:**
Ask yourself what you are going to learn from meeting this challenge. If you have lost someone or your home, then focus on what you gained from knowing that person or living in that place. There is a difference between authentically experiencing negative emotions and moving through them in good time and getting stuck revisiting past hurts and losses again and again. Sometimes people become addicted to doing this, rather than face the challenge of creating meaning in the present moment and setting intentions for the future. This is a cop-out and not the best way to win friends and influence people.

Three key strategies can help with reframing your attitude:

a) **Put the stressor in perspective**
Ask yourself: How bad is this situation? Will I lose my life or my loved ones? Will I go broke? Will I starve? Will I lose my job?

b) **Shift your focus**
This is essentially the idea of panning for gold, rather than swimming around in the mud. We can focus in on the worst aspects of a situation or what might happen. We can catastrophize things. This process simply reinforces neural patterns in the mind that churn up negative emotions unnecessarily. Creating a Gratitude List as we did in the daily practice exercises in Principle One can help.

49

c) Use the difficulty

In my work in the theatre, people sometimes talk about the principle of use the difficulty. In a television interview on Parkinson (you can look it up on You Tube), famous UK actor Sir Michael Caine tells the story from when he was a young actor rehearsing a scene. There was a couple on stage acting out an argument and a chair got thrown and blocked his entrance onto the set.

Sir Michael says:

I opened the door, and I said to the director, 'I can't get in. There's a chair in my way.' He said, 'Well, use the difficulty. If it's a drama, pick it up and smash it. If it's a comedy, fall over it.' This was a principle I took into my own life: always use the difficulty. I tell my children there's never anything so bad where you can't get something out of a situation. If we use it only a quarter of one percent to our advantage, then we're ahead. We didn't let it get us down. Use the difficulty.

EXERCISE:

Work on two stressors you are dealing with at this time:

	What did I tell myself and others that created more drama than necessary in this situation?	When did I handle similar situations in the past? What did I do then? What did I say to myself that helped?	What will I learn from this situation? How can I use the difficulty?
Stressor 1			
Stressor 2			

A checklist of ways to improve your resilience in stressful situations:

1. **Get more exercise:**
   - 20 mins, three times week until I'm out of breath and perspiring (please check with a doctor first to get the OK!)

2. **Improve your diet:**
   - reduced caffeine intake, less sugar, less salt, less fast-burning carbohydrates, less cholesterol (please check with a doctor)

3. **Increase your daily practice:**
   - yoga, meditation, progressive muscle relaxation

4. **Take short breaks:**
   - take a short walk, visit the stress management cubicle, walk slowly and deliberately somewhere for 5 minutes practising presence

5. **Breathing exercises:**
   - as we covered in daily practice in Principle One; see below

6. **Reduce toxicity:**
   - ration your time on digital devices if you can; get out into nature, surrounded by plants and trees in a pollution-free environment; take a different route or time to and from work

7. **Work organisation:**
   - our brains are simply not equipped to deal with the amount of stimulations they get in our modern lives. Try to:
     - Improve your skills in the systems and equipment you use
     - Declutter your workspaces: physical and digital
     - Create overview of the important areas of focus and tasks
     - Create easy, efficient electronic and physical storage systems
     - Only work on one thing at a time
     - Use digital devices/check emails at set times in the day

The five-step breathing technique: your circuit breaker

Having an immediate "circuit breaker" practice can help reduce sudden increases in stress. You can do this mini-workout anywhere as it's quite subtle, although if you can get away from a stressful situation, you are more likely to be able to get some altitude on a demanding situation and respond in a healthier way.

The idea is to work through one group of muscles at a time, clenching them, then relaxing, while breathing deeply and steadily. This can quickly reduce your level of tension and help you shift down a gear as you go through the day.

Breath 1: **Breathe in deeply and out again fully, feeling your stomach move; unclench your jaw...and relax as you breathe out.**

Breath 2: Clench your feet muscles as you breathe in...and relax as you breathe out.

Breath 3: Clench your hands and the upper parts of your body as you breathe in...and relax as you breathe out.

Breath 4: Clench your jaw as you breathe in...and relax as you breathe out.

Breath 5: Clench your stomach as you breathe in...and relax as you breathe out.

Take it easy, take it easy
Don't let the sound of your own wheels
Drive you crazy
Lighten up while you still can
Don't even try to understand
Just find a place to make your stand
And take it easy...

The Eagles

PRINCIPLE 3
References and further reading

[1] www.mit-online.getsmarter.com/presentations/lp/mit-sloan-neuroscience-for-business-online-short-course/

[2] The Source: Open Your Mind, Change Your Life; Dr Tara Swart; Ebury Digital; 2019

[3] www.medicalnewstoday.com/articles/321060#other-brain-myths

[4] Drubach, Daniel. The Brain Explained. New Jersey: Prentice-Hall, 2000.

[5] www.usgs.gov/special-topics/water-science-school/science/water-you-water-and-human-body

[6] The Hidden Life of Trees, Peter Wohlleben: Greystone Kids; 2016

[7] www.thehealthsite.com/diseases-conditions/10-health-hazards-of-mobile-phones-139726/

[8] Wu, B. Social isolation and loneliness among older adults in the context of COVID-19: a global challenge. glob health res policy 5, 27 (2020). https://doi.org/10.1186/s41256-020-00154-3; https://rdcu.be/cSTC9

For any thoughts or feelings...

_____

_____

_____

_____

_____

_____

_____

_____

_____

_____

PRINCIPLE 4
BE INTENTIONAL

Where am I headed?
What is my intention?

When we set clear intentions, we are activating our mental, physical, and emotional resources to move towards a clear picture of the future we want to create.

The best way to predict your future is to invent it

Alan Kay

When you daydream, it is like watching a Facebook® feed, or some TikTok® videos. You see a range of images, hear sounds, and even experience emotions, one after another.

When we allow this to happen, this can give us a natural ability to tune into the deeper drivers of our lives and see positive pictures of the future.

At worst, we can abuse this ability and start ruminating over past hurts and resentments, often using our imaginations to add to the story: "He was trying to... She was only interested in... How could they have treated me this way?" When we do this we are setting an amplified feedback loop between our thoughts and our feelings, trapping us in the past in our shallow self.

Learning from the past is important, as is grieving properly over the loss of a loved one, for example, but recycling over and over again and embellishing our baggage can keep us stuck in the past – or swimming around in the mud, to reuse our metaphor.

When we're looking for the gold in the present moment and setting intentions for the future, we can certainly use our imaginations as a powerful tool to help us clarify our picture of perfection. Then we need to structure our planning to move in the right direction, especially the coming 24-48 hours. Get these clear and under control, then we can use more general overviews of longer time periods ahead (see Principle Five).

Digital toxicity

The problem with using technology to stimulate our imagination, even though we may believe we're just passing time, is that we are often getting over-stimulated with too many diverse ideas that are not related to the present moment.

We might simply burn up our mental resources, moving from one idea to another at high speed, without experiencing any topic or moment deeply. We might see the odd fleck of gold to keep us hooked but nothing rich, rewarding, or deeply satisfying.

How often have you put your devices down after a long period of surfing and felt a sense of dissatisfaction?

By practicing the art of presence, and allowing ourselves to visualize, we can start to access our Deeper Self and get some inspired clarity on the future we'd like to aim to create. Even if we never arrive in the precise point we aim for, we have created opportunities to build relationships, learn things, and create positive memories.

By dreaming of our possible future, we can set a direction for our lives. We can actively imagine what achieving our goals will look, sound, and feel like. The more we practise visualizing the outcomes we are aiming for the more powerful these thoughts become.

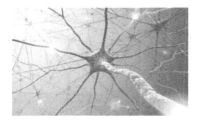

Modern studies of neuroscience show us that by doing this, we are creating and strengthening various new neural pathways that will shape our day-to-day choices. It's as if we are setting up our internal navigation system that will help guide us to our chosen destination.

Most people want to hear or tell a good story. But they don't realize they can and should be the good story. That requires intentional living

John C. Maxwell

Of course, this works both ways. If we ruminate over resentments and regrets too much, we will strengthen these neural pathways and start to live in a world that echoes these perceptions and feelings about other people.

Whichever way we decide to practise using our minds, by shaping these neural pathways we become primed to spot opportunities to move towards them when they arise: a chance meeting with someone who can help us, a learning event we spot, a notice board with a clue...

An easy demonstration is if I ask you, for the next five minutes, not to think about a big pink giraffe. It doesn't mean you will meet one but if you walk past someone wearing pink in a crowd, or a child with a toy giraffe, you will more likely find your attention drawn to it.

Vision boards

One great method for setting your intention is to create a vision board – either for yourself, with your partner, or even with a work team. It's a technique often used by brand designers to identify a style and tone for a brand. I've used these many times over the years for brand and culture projects as well as for personal intention setting - alone, or with other people.

You create a board full of carefully chosen images, words, and short sayings that you can look at every day. You create one and then spend time focusing on the images and how they make you feel.

Some would say that doing this will attract chance situations in your life that reflect the feelings you feel during the exercise. It's as if you start to create small coincidences that seem to be signposting you in the right direction.

I heard a lovely saying about intention setting recently:

Live more from intention and less from habit

Amy Rubin Flet

The process here is to sense your true and best intentions consciously, then imagine it happening and keep believing it can and will happen. This process is more than just wishful thinking of course. If we keep visualizing the outcome(s) we are aiming for, keep believing, keep looking for opportunities to move forward, no matter how small, then we strengthen the neural pathways.

This means we will be ready to grasp the right opportunities as and when they seem to pop up, one by one. Our intentions will turn into concrete reality as we take advantage of these pleasant surprises.

You can set an intention for your life, for a project, even one piece of work at a time. If you have a presentation to make, set the intention for:

- How it's going to go
- How people will feel about it
- What they will do with what you share
- What you want your audience to take away at the end
- What you want them to think, feel, and do after hearing what you have to say

How can vision boards help? There are two good reasons to use this great tool:

1. Our mind responds more strongly to visual stimulation
When you create a vision board and put it where you see it often, you are automatically revisiting your intentions and rewiring the neural pathways in your brain.

2. Visualisation is a way of actually wiring your brain
When you are visualizing, you are consciously teaching the brain new thought processes. Your brain will work tirelessly to achieve the messages that you feed your subconscious.

The first step is knowing what you want - the real results you want to achieve. What are your dreams, priorities, goals? Why do you get out of bed each morning? What is your purpose and what makes you feel alive? Then once you have answers to these questions, you can develop a plan of the actions and tasks that will move you in the right direction. How will you spend your time, money, and energy? Are you spending time doing what matters most to you? If not, what do you need to change?

The first step is to establish that something is possible, then probability will occur
Elon Musk

How do I make a vision board?

This can be done on your own, or perhaps with your partner, other members of the family, or even colleagues if you want to create one for a team, product, brand, or service.

1. Spend time gathering screenshots or scans of images from magazines, Instagram, Facebook, blogs, or motivational sayings. Collect pictures of images that make you happy or inspire a good feeling. Get hold of a large board – a cork noticeboard works, or some board from an art shop.

2. Prepare by spending some time doing the Presence meditations that we mentioned earlier. Perhaps play some music you really like. You can even make a ritual out of the process, take a shower, put on some suitable clothing, perhaps light some candles.

3. Daydream and allow yourself to play your own movie of your present and future life. Think about the important people in your life – your family and friends. Who would you like to attract into your life? Name the qualities of each person. Think about your strengths, your purpose, your principles, your work...

4. Select the images, sayings and keywords. Slowly fill out the board with carefully handpicked items that each represent an intention in your life. Review. Make sure you spend time each day or week looking back over the board and reminding yourself of the intention you have set. At the end of a day or week, write down all the details of any progress you've made towards the future state you want to create. This will keep signalling to the brain that you mean business and want its help!

Performance standards

You may want to consider setting some performance standards that specify precisely what you want to strive to achieve. An athlete may aspire to win an Olympic gold medal but may need to achieve a clear standard of performance on a given day in order to make the dream a reality.

Applying performance standards on the way to your goals can help determine the effort you need to make and add a fun and healthy element of challenge.

If you are looking to retire, how much money will you need and by when? If you are building your own business, what are the key sales and expense targets you will work towards?

Chunking

Often, we find ourselves facing a mountain-sized task. We procrastinate, postpone, make another coffee, arrange to see a friend – anything but getting down to it!

A really good technique here is to chunk the task down to its smallest components and focus on short-term progress. What can you do in the next 24-48 hours, that is a small bite out of the huge bar of chocolate - so big you feel sick looking at it!

- Learn a language = six new words each day Monday thru' Friday, and read a chapter of a book on Wednesdays.

- Get fitter = a 15-minute brisk walk four days this week.

- Tackle a long-term project = 30 mins a day this week on research.

The Story of John Nabers

John Nabers was a good club swimmer at best. In 1972, he was watching Mark Spitz win seven gold medals. John's event was the 100 metres backstroke and he thought "Imagine winning the gold medal at the next Olympics?"

The winning time for his event was 56.3 seconds. John worked out that he would need to swim in the final at a time of 55.5 seconds to be likely to win the race. His current time was 59.5 - four whole seconds slower. The idea of shaving four whole seconds off his time was way too daunting. So, he started chunking...

He had four years to lose four seconds, which was one second per year. This was 1/12th of a second per month, or 1/300th of a second a day (allowing 65 rest days in a year) . He would train for two hours twice a day, so this made his intention to average an improvement of 1/600th for every training session. A blink of an eye is 1/3rd of a second. To shave four seconds off a time for a 100m sprint is a huge mountain, whereas to shave off 0.005% of a blink of an eye per training session is a grain of sand...or gold.

The Olympic records show that the gold medal for the 100 metres backstroke at the Montreal Olympics in 1976 was won by John Nabers in a time of 55.49!

Just one hundredth of a second faster than the time he had predicted four years earlier. He could have even had a few more days off!

Don't just constantly aim for some kind of distant idea of a future. If you enjoy the process each day you'll be making your dream come true.

David Bowie

The Man Who Planted Trees*

The Man Who Planted Trees is a short story written for the magazine Reader's Digest in 1953 by Jean Giono. It describes the life's work of Elzéard Bouffier, a solitary shepherd who breathes life into the entire eco-system of an area of desert - by planting trees.

The story has inspired films, theatre productions and publication into many languages. Giono chose to make his work royalty-free in order to inspire a love of nature and the environment in as many people as possible.

In 1913, a young man is travelling alone on a hiking trip through Provence, France, and into the Alps, enjoying the relatively unspoiled wilderness. He runs out of water in a treeless, desolate valley where only wild lavender grows and there is no trace of civilization except old, empty crumbling buildings.

He finds only a dried-up well but is saved by a middle-aged shepherd who takes him to a spring that flows with fresh water.

Curious about this man and why he has chosen such a lonely life, the narrator stays with him for a time. The shepherd's name is Elzéard Bouffier. He explains that after being widowed, he decided to restore the ruined landscape of this isolated and largely abandoned area by cultivating a forest, bit by bit, by planting acorns. He makes holes in the ground with his straight iron staff and drops acorns in them that he has collected from many miles away. He also grows beech and birch saplings for planting.

Little by little, he plants a few trees every day. He knows that some will die or fall prey to disease, but he keeps working away, day after day.

The narrator leaves the shepherd, returns home, and later fights in the First World War. In 1920, shell-shocked and depressed after the war, the man returns. He is surprised to see young saplings of all forms taking root in the valley and new streams running through it, where the shepherd has even created a number of dams higher up in the mountains to provide water for this new eco-system.

The narrator makes a full recovery in the peace and beauty of the regrowing valley and continues to visit the region and his friend every year. He even finds on one visit that Bouffier is no longer a shepherd. The sheep were eating his young trees, so he has moved on to become a bee keeper instead.

The valley receives official protection after the First World War, with the French authorities mistakenly believing that the rapid growth of the new forest is a bizarre natural phenomenon. They know nothing of Bouffier's selfless work. Over four decades he continues to plant trees and the valley gradually flourishes into a kind of Garden of Eden, rich in diversity and new life.

By the end of the story the valley is vibrant with life and is peacefully settled with more than 10,000 people living there, unaware that they owe their happiness to Bouffier. The narrator tells one of his friends, a government forester, the truth about the new forest and the friend also takes on a mission to try to help protect it.

In 1945 the narrator visits the now very old Bouffier one last time.

In 1947 in a hospice in Banon the man who planted trees peacefully passes away, but his beautiful creation lives on, and on...

Planting trees may be the single most important ecotechnology that we have to put the broken pieces of our planet back together.

Jim Robbins, The Man Who Planted Trees: Lost Groves

Processes

Once you set your goals, you need to create some processes to ensure you do what you need to do to achieve them...at the right time.

If you can't describe what you are doing as a process, you don't know what you are doing
W. Edwards Deming

You may dream of being able to retire from working by the age of 60 with sufficient funds to support your new life. This may include paying off a mortgage, so you may want to schedule milestones and mortgage reviews along the way. You may want to initiate some research into different types of pensions and other investments such as ISAs and other places where your money will grow...hopefully.

You may want to map out a timetable for repaying car loans and setting up your own business venture. You will want to be vibrant and healthy when you retire, so what are the fitness and nutrition processes you need?

Effectively you are looking at breaking down your overall intentions into smaller units. Each unit brings you one step closer to arriving at the destination you have set your intentions on.

If you lead a project, what processes do you need to set up? What are the key initiatives you need to take, with who and when? How will you communicate these plans? How will you develop each individual and the team culture as a whole?

Clear processes help make you a gold miner, not a mud swimmer.

Using intentional language

When you are thinking and talking about your intentions:

- Do you find it easy to find the words that accurately communicate what you want to achieve?
- Do you ever feel like when you say something, it's not really what you mean?
- Do you sometimes walk away from an intense conversation feeling worked up, overwhelmed, or defeated?
- Do you ever indulge in self-defeating, internal speak versus self-affirming, intentional speak?

Self-defeating, internal	Self-affirming, intentional
I'm too young/too old	I will learn how to do it
No-one listens to me	I will be clear and impactful
I'm not qualified to speak	I can talk about what I do know
I'm not a numbers person	I can get help with the calculations
I don't know how	I will figure this out
I'll try to fit it in	I will do it...or...I won't do it
He/she always ruins things	I will manage these situations better

Can you think of some examples of self-defeating speak you hear around you? What would be more self-affirming and intentional?

_____   _____

_____   _____

When you use intentional language, you're communicating clear messages to yourself and others. You're saying what you mean and meaning what you say, while remaining emotionally detached enough not to react to the way others respond to you if they don't give you the response you are looking for. This doesn't give us carte blanche to say anything to anyone we want. Honesty without tact can easily become cruelty.

Our goal is to use clear and effective, intentional language that lets us and other people know where we stand and what our motives are, what we need, and of course, how we will help them out as well.

What is the difference between saying a) and b) to someone? What sense of intention do you get from each version?

a) Do you need any help?

and:
b) What help can I give you?

_____

How about the difference between...

a) I will try to do it when I can.

and:
b) I will do it by Monday.

_____

Case study – Intentional communication

It is mid-morning.
You are busy working at a desk in the office on an important project with a deadline for the end of today. Last week, you emailed Bertie for some information he has that you need to include in the document you have to send in by the end of the day. Two months ago, he was late delivering some other material and it caused some panic for you and your team.

Which of these thoughts and emotions might you be having?

- I wonder what happened with Bertie? I hope he's OK.
- Oh-oh. Here we go again! Just like last time.
- It's always about him. He is such a *******.

What if we added some more information: You find Bertie quite self-centered. He only seems interested in what's happening in his world. You don't particularly like him.

Which of these thoughts and emotions might you be having?

- I wonder what happened Bertie? I hope he's OK.
- Oh-oh. Here we go again! Just like last time.
- It's always about him. He is such a *******.

What if we added even more information? Bertie was promoted with a big pay rise and a company car three months ago for a post you had applied for.

Which of these thoughts and emotions might you be having?

- I wonder what happened Bertie? I hope he's OK.
- Oh-oh. Here we go again! Just like last time.
- It's always about him. He is such a *******.

We often think we're communicating in a clear and intentional way, when in truth we are being triggered by our own shallow-self reactions to the story we are creating about our experiences.

Being intentional requires:

1. Self-awareness: **Check your body, mind, emotions. What is happening in your body? How is your breathing rate? Where is there tension in the body? What thoughts are you focusing on? Are you overdoing the "stinking thinking"?**

2. Take a time-out: **Before we react, you need to:**

1. Stop
2. Breathe
3. Refocus on intention
4. Choose the right action

You must work with Nancy to get things done, so your intention is to cultivate a positive working relationship with her.

3. De-contaminate your language: **It's so easy to leak our reactive, egoic reactions through our choice of words and/or subject matter. A subtle slap is so easy to slide out there with our choice of words:**

"Nancy, I'm pleased you can do this today...after the last time."

4. Emotional reality checks: **Name your feelings.** Are your feelings about what is happening in the present moment, or are there some past stories of other people and situations that are adding to the intensity? Is there some old baggage repeating itself?

Being intentional with digital distractions

Deloitte Insights[1] has published numerous studies that reveal how students consistently choose multitasking - turning their attention to something else and back again - over remaining focused on a single task in hand. Even if the task is something very important, they just can't resist the urge to switch between activities.

In one study[2], third-year college students volunteered to have their laptops monitored. They spent 42 percent of their time on other activities, with an average of 65 open and active windows on their laptop monitor during a lecture; 63 percent of those windows were for non-course-related activities (gaming, emails, web surfing, and entertainment). Students were basically flipping their focus between multiple activities at any given time.

What do you recognise of this behaviour in yourself and others?

_____

_____

Are you being accurate in assessing yourself? This study also showed that these students underestimated how much this was happening - instant messaging by 40 percent and email usage by 7 percent.[3]

Another study[4] of more than 1,000 college students revealed 80 percent admitting to texting during class; 15 percent of the group were sending 11 or more text messages during a single class session.

The report concluded with a summary of research findings to highlight the impact of this lack of focus and intentionality:

- Work takes longer
- Quality of your work suffers
- Ability to remember what is learnt falls
- Future application of the learning is more difficult

According to workplace advisors SHRM[5], a survey of 3,750 knowledge workers conducted by Workfront found that the workers were interrupted by e-mail, instant messages, and other digital distractions nearly 14 times per day on average.

Another survey SHRM quote is from Adobe[5], who found that the average U.S. office worker spends more than three hours each day trying to keep up with work e-mail. And an analysis of data from 50,000 workers collected by Rescue Time, a Seattle-based company that tracks digital activities, showed that the average knowledge worker goes only six minutes without checking in with one or more digital tools.

That same study revealed that 40 minutes was the longest amount of time the average worker could go without checking e-mail during the workday. Forty percent never managed 30 straight minutes of focused work time.

Being intentional with digital technology

There are some powerful habits to cultivate that will help you become more intentional at work and at home.

Clean the clutter from your phone and desktop/laptop screens: they should appear organized and positive to look at, not with an endless menu of distractions. Have cool images that inspire you and remind you of the importance of being present and experiencing real life, not just digital life. Put apps into folders to clean up the overview. Get rid of older, redundant apps and data. Do the same with physical files.

Keep your tabs shut: only use the ones that relate to what you are working on in this period.

Move devices and other things you are not using out of sight: create an area of single-minded, conscious focus. As the old saying goes: Out of sight is out of mind. We can only fully concentrate on one new and important thing at a time. Yes, we can juggle a few familiar things when we drive a car, or preparing a meal we've cooked before, but if we're taking a new route through the mountains or a working on a new cordon bleu dish - these will need our total concentration. Clear your workspace and put anything that might distract you out of sight.

Turn notifications OFF: be more intentional by working to planned times to review emails and check messages – after lunch, after coffee, when you return from a meeting. If you need to learn to spend less time on social media, this will help. You won't be checking notifications every minute of the day. You won't be dropping everything at the sight of an icon or sound of a bell. You'll be doing it intentionally, productively, and deliberately.

Being intentional with digital technology - contd

Take regular breaks: take planned, complete breaks from digital media every few hours and do an activity that brings you into presence with your environment. A walk in a park, time on a beach, doing a practical activity with a friend or family member, some exercise (without ear pod music!). Spend time being who you really are in the present moment to still your mind and deepen your connection with being alive - here and now. Fear of missing out on digital devices is nothing compared to missing out on quality relationships with loved ones. Set a cut-off time every day/evening and do something with your family or other half. Minimise your time in the online world when you're on holiday.

Digital media can be useful tools;
they're not meant to be our way of life

Actions for me:

_____

_____

_____

_____

_____

_____

PRINCIPLE 4
References and further reading

[1] www2.deloitte.com/uk/en/insights/focus/behavioral-economics/managing-digital-distractions-in-workplace.html

[2] J.M. Kraushaar and D.C. Novak, "Examining the effects of student multitasking with laptops during the lecture," Journal of Information Systems Education 21, no. 2, pp. 241–251.

[3] Whittemore School of Business and Economics, University of New Hampshire, "In-class texting behaviors of college students: A university-wide study to determine the in-class texting attitudes and behaviors of students at the University of New Hampshire," http://www.unh.edu/news/docs/UNHtextingstudy.pdf, accessed November 4, 2014.

[4] Jeff Sovern, "Law student laptop use during class for non-class purposes: Temptation v. incentives," University of Louisville Law Review 51, no. 3 (2013): pp. 483–534

[5] www.shrm.org/ResourcesAndTools/hr-topics/technology/ Pages/Reducing-Digital-Distractions-at-Work.aspx

For any thoughts or feelings...

_____

_____

_____

_____

_____

_____

_____

_____

_____

ORGANISE YOUR THOUGHTS & COMMUNICATIONS

Working and communicating in a clear, structured way.

It is important to view knowledge as sort of a semantic tree - make sure you understand the fundamental principles; the trunk and big branches, before you get into the leaves/details or there is nothing for them to hang on to

Elon Musk

As Elon Musk reminds us, we need some structure and control to turn intentions into actions. We've talked about how you need to be clear on your purpose (the why behind your what) and your values (the way you do things) and your intentions (the what) before you get into the detail (the how) of how you will use the most valuable resource we have - time - to bear fruit, to create positive impacts for ourselves and others.

We can use our tree structure to create an overview, to consider all our priorities, and then to build a bridge between our intentions and some of the concrete things we need to do to move forward successfully. You can use one big piece of paper to map out a vision board for your next 1-3 years, then another to map out all the branches and twigs of your life and where you will need to focus your energies.

This will help your brain see the road ahead much more clearly in terms of the choices you need to make with the time you have available, after you have factored in all of the less negotiable commitments that are driven by other people and your responsibilities at work and home.

71

Here is an example of how you might use a tree structure to turn an intention, like being happy and healthy, into executable tasks. When we map out our plans this way, we can create an overview that also gives us a checklist we can use to control how we use the time we have available.

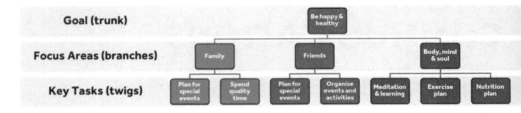

We can create a tree for each major goal. Once this is done, we have a decision structure to look at how to prioritize tasks for the time we have available to us. This process can be done personally, or with team mates and even family.

- What are the real results I/we are aiming for in the next xyz months/years?

- What areas will we need to focus on to achieve these things?

- What concrete steps will we need to take: who, what, where and when?

You can use sticky notes to list all the things you have to do and want to do to turn your intentions (goals) into action.

You can then group them together under headings. You can create your own for each key intention you have set in life.

Then you can introduce daily, weekly, monthly and annual reviews of progress and resets for the period ahead.

How to prioritize: The Eisenhower Matrix

Most priorities we have in life fall into one of four types:

TYPE 1: Tasks that are of high urgency **and** high importance.

For example:
- Leaving the building in a fire
- Dealing with a customer who has just called in a crisis
- Helping a sick family member
- Your manager needs you right now

My examples:

_____

_____

TYPE 2: Tasks that are lower urgency **and** high importance.

For example:
- Implementing a new fitness and diet program
- Starting a big project that needs to be completed next year
- Learning Spanish
- Spending quality time with family and close friends

My examples:

_____

_____

TYPE 2 tasks are the important things we need to do to realise our intentions. But in many cases they do not appear so urgent so we can too easily postpone them for TYPE 3 or TYPE 4 tasks. Spending time regularly, and being ahead of time on these tasks, is a more proactive approach which will make life seem less urgent in general. Often, they include critical things that concern the kind of future we wish to manifest and will be the keytasks that move us in our chosen direction.

73

Further examples of TYPE 2 tasks are developing, leveraging, and sustaining our business networks (our ecosystem); coaching people in our team to increase the contributions they can make; important project work; and personal development. You need to intentionally allocate time for these each day to keep things progressing. This will help create a situation where fewer tasks feel urgent and you feel more in control.

TYPE 3: Tasks that often appear urgent, but are of lower importance.

For example:

- Answering an email where someone is asking for some information
- Responding to a friend asking if you are free for a meal next month
- Responding to a colleague who just arrives at your desk for a chat
- Checking for messages on your phone that pop up

Some of these activities can wait for you to attend to TYPE 1 tasks and to make some progress at least on TYPE 2 to ensure you are taking some chunks out of these. You may find that some TYPE 3 tasks are in fact only someone else's priority! Are they really urgent, or can you agree a longer deadline, or even find a way to delegate them? TYPE 3 can be routine tasks with a deadline that impacts on others such as daily administration.

They may also include tasks that may belong to someone else but have been passed onto you with or without your consent. Such tasks can seem like emergencies but the urgency may belong to others. They are urgent but not high value to you in the context of the real results you are aiming to achieve, so you need to balance how much time you are investing in these at the expense of TYPE 1 and TYPE 2 tasks.

My examples:

_____

_____

As we develop our life skills, we can look for creative ways of delegating some TYPE 3 tasks that so easily eat up our available time.

- Who is better placed to do this task better than me?
- How can I cultivate the support I need to get more done?
- How can I make sure I recognize the people who do things that keep my life on track?

How I can delegate some TYPE 3 tasks:

_____

_____

TYPE 4: Tasks that are less urgent and are of lower importance.

For example:
- Buy some new clothes for next summer
- Check the football results
- Eat junk food
- Clean your car

My examples:

_____

_____

This is often where you can find yourself swimming in the mud if you are avoiding things that are more challenging. TYPE 4 tasks are still important but not as important as making progress on the others - particularly TYPE 1 and 2. Sometimes it's easier to do the more mundane tasks instead of important things. Being intentional means coaching ourselves with questions such as: Why am I doing this? What is it helping me achieve? Is there a better way? Can I eliminate some of these?

Of course, if some of these types of tasks are not completed at some point, they can become urgent and important. So we may need to put time into our plan to get them done. We can use part of the day when we know we are not at our most productive, so we need less mental capacity to get it done - after lunch or in between meetings, for example.

The Eisenhower Matrix is a well-used time and resource management system that helps you see which tasks are top priority and which can wait, using company goals and your personal intentions as the filter.

If we don't schedule Type 2 tasks in our daily plans, we will endlessly be working on things that are urgent! This is not being in control.

Being intentional is about using the exact same hours that everyone else has in a much more effective way...

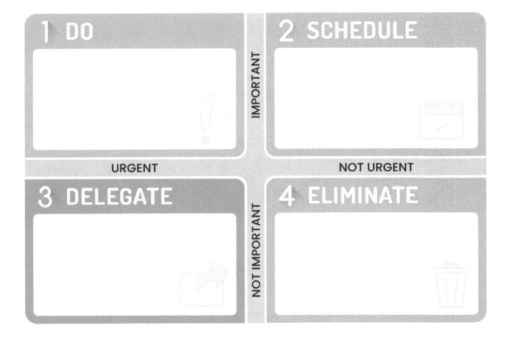

By categorising your tasks using this framework, you can make much more mindful choices about how you can use the time you have. Let's face it, we all have the same 24 hours a day, 7 days a week, 365 days a year.

The tools in this book can help you become much more effective in deciding how you spend each day. Setting intentions are just the basis for moving in a certain direction. Even if we don't get all the way there, we can certainly find some golden nuggets along the way.

Making well-structured presentations

Why do people disengage with many presentations?

Given the amount of digital distraction we are being exposed to, winning other peoples' attention is an art in itself. Get good at this and your road to achieving results will open up much wider.

Do you have to make presentations in your role? Are you likely to in the future? Do you volunteer when the opportunity comes up, or do you head for the stress management cubicle or look for something on the floor as soon as the subject is raised?

In my experience, there are not good and bad presenters per se. There are people who come fully alive when they address people online or in-person, and they create a flowing, engaging, and positive message, and there are people who speak as walking automatons or just shrink away under the pressure of the performance by reading out lists of bullet points from slides.

In my Speaker Coaching (www.soulcorporations.com/speak-with-soul/) sessions, I use all my speaking experience, coupled with my career as a theatre and TV director-producer to help participants develop their competencies in the following:

- Structuring a presentation
- Using rhetoric
- Telling stories
- Turning nerves into vibrant energy
- Developing authentic presence
- Handling difficult situations
- Becoming a thought leader-influencer
- Presenting in an on-brand way

In some of these programmes, we've had a lot of fun doing them entirely online as well as using a West End theatre space.

We often get people presenting without slides. This is because we've found that the most important vehicles in communicating messages are what you say, the way you say it, and your non-verbal communications (see Presence exercises in Principle One). So often, we see people really letting themselves down by relying too heavily on poor or busy slides.

77

When you are grounded in your core purpose; present in body, mind, heart and soul; crystal-clear on your intention for the presentation and the value you want people to obtain from listening to you; and ready with a well-structured plan for your presentation, you will be great.

If you are using a few slides to add impact and memorability, then this is a good thing. But slides are not aide memoires for you alone. They can offer focal points for you to elaborate on in your speech with colourful examples, but never a complicated list to read out in detail! If you have a lot of detail to share, use handouts rather than busy and tiresome slides.

A simple method for creating structured and inspiring communication

Inspiring people requires the inner qualities of calmness, confidence, and authenticity. To develop these, you need to take steps to become fully grounded in the body and have a crystal-clear structure around which to base the communication. Getting this combination right can result in a message that is relevant and resonates with your audience on a personal level. This is what will inspire people to want to listen.

Research has shown that people are often affected by emotional contagion when they are with others who are experiencing emotion. Think of a football match, a sad film, or an uplifting music performance. People can feel what a presenter feels. We can use this as a powerful tool or at worst be victims of it if we don't prepare.

By asking yourself why a few times, you can access your deeper motivations for your presentation. For example, you are asked to present a new accounting process:

Why do I care about this?
It's important the company knows its financial position month to month.

Why do I care about this?
I want to help the company be successful.

Why do I care about this?
People value being part of a successful company. It helps improve their job security and creates the opportunities for satisfying work.

Why do I really care about this?
Because I want to help people improve their quality of life.

You can follow this method for your next presentation:

Presentation Title: _____

Why do I care about this?

_____

Why do I care about this?

_____

Why do I really care about this?

_____

Why should the audience want to listen?

_____

How will I get peoples' attention at the beginning?

_____

How will I show them I know them?

_____

When I have finished speaking, my audience will take away:

_____

_____

The first action step I want them to take:

_____

How will I keep them engaged?

_____

Structuring your communications

When you are fully grounded in the purpose and intentions you have for your communication/presentation, you can start to get creative about the content:

- Using small sticky notes write down lots of ideas for what you could include, one idea at a time, one or two words per sticky note. Include a key point you want to make, an example, and questions you might want to raise to get people thinking about the content.

- When you feel you have enough start to move these sticky notes around the page until you can see headings emerge to group all the elements.

- Then you can create an introduction where you can introduce the purpose, describe the agenda (the headings), and then flow smoothly through the elements, summarising and calling people to act.

INTRODUCTION	HEADING 1	HEADING 2	HEADING 3	SUMMARY/FINISH
KEY QUESTION/ STORY/PHRASE	KEY QUESTION/ STORY/PHRASE			REVIEW/QUESTIONS
HEADING 1 etc	KEY POINT EXAMPLE			CALL TO ACTION
				BIG FINISH

When you have completed this and have a clear structure to follow, then you can see if any slides might help add clarity, impact, and/or memorability to your presentation.

If you can't explain it simply, you don't understand it well enough
Albert Einstein

PRINCIPLE 6
CULTIVATE MINDFUL INTERACTIONS

What are the positive interactions I need to have with the key people in my life?

In one drop of water are found all the secrets of all the oceans; in one aspect of you are found all the aspects of existence

Kahlil Gibran Jr.

Forests are often the result of many trees working together. They are interwoven and interdependent. When we walk in an older forest, it has a noticeably calming effect and can provide rest and relaxation. This is a very creative, natural system that is in harmony and is highly productive and resilient. We can learn from trees and we need to look after them.

Water is a transparent, tasteless, odourless chemical substance. And while it is essential for all forms of life, it actually provides no nutrition in itself. Since water makes up about half of a tree's composition, it plays a central role in how a tree accesses the nutrients in the soil and the energy from the sun in photosynthesis. Water can enter the t ooh ree through its roots and leaves. Water evaporates via this same route, eventually returning to the rivers and lakes as rain. There is a constant, positive, reciprocal conversation happening that helps each tree grow to its full potential.

This metaphor points us towards the value of cultivating positive relationships with people whose support we value. And of course this needs to be based on a spirit of give-and-take, and most importantly, in our global community we need to do more than just embrace diversity; we need to delight in it if we are to achieve positive results together.

Looking through the prism...

Delighting in diversity

How can diversity help a business sharpen its competitive edge by helping people who are different to combine successfully? How can we focus on our similarities while respecting our differences?

Great teams often have a diversity of strengths
with a similarity of spirit
Mike Pegg[1]

In many sports, understanding and embracing diversity is a vital ingredient to create a competitive advantage. Many sports were originally created to include people of different body shapes and capabilities to make sure everyone got some exercise! I was relatively full-figured as a teenager but not so tall, so I was a prop forward when I played rugby. In a rugby scrum, these are the people in the front row who bear the weight of the entire eight forwards shoving together.

Rugby would be the perfect metaphor for looking at the value of diversity if we ignored its history of excluding women and people living with disability. Not so much today, of course. Much progress has been made. Women's rugby and disability rugby are both now thriving as positive human eco-systems.

The drive for diversity and inclusion in sport intensified recently in County Cricket following the Azeem Rafiq racism scandal in Yorkshire in the UK. West Indies fast bowler Michael Holding has also been a pioneer in helping bring the issues of racial inclusion to the forefront of modern sport. We've seen footballers taking the knee before matches in a statement that says: 'Black lives matter.'

Organisations are focusing on Diversity, Equity and Inclusion more than ever before as we move in a more positive direction as a human race.

Valuing neurodiversity

We need to work together to get things right. But how about the value of another form of diversity: neurodiversity? This is a much more subtle and hidden form of diversity. It also relates to people living with ADHD, Asperger's, autism, Tourette's and other more recognisable conditions.

Let's face the facts: we are each of us unique. Each of our brains is wired uniquely as gazillions of brain cells fire off in response to the unique experiences of our lives and form the neural pathways we use to navigate and interact with our worlds. Each set of life experiences, including more profound experiences such as conflict and facing up to major challenges or even trauma, create new neural pathways that shape our perceptions of others and our reactions to them in later life.

The good news, fortunately, is that the science is revealing that we can literally change the way our brains work; we can rewire ourselves!

We can establish new neural pathways that shift our perceptions and responses to one another. By consciously focusing on and reworking the way we think about ourselves and other people, we can literally change the world we experience and how we deal with others. So how can learning to value neurodiversity lead us to lead better lives in a modern workplace?

Gillian Lynne

One area is how we recognise our own and others' talent. The late Sir Ken Robinson[2] argued that our schools can kill creativity. Our standardised approaches often exclude many talented young people who learn in many different ways. His lovely example of how the great dancer and choreographer Gillian Lynne was taken to a psychiatrist in her early years as she wouldn't sit still in class and was seen as a problem child, rather than the star she became after the psychiatrist interpreted her behaviour as latent talent and recommended she was taken to a dance school. As Robinson points out, "ADHD hadn't been invented yet. It wasn't an available condition. Nobody knew they could have that...in our modern era, a young Gillian would probably be given medication and told to calm down."

83

In the modern workplace, things can be seen very differently by people who are wired differently. And in a modern organisation not only is it politically and morally correct to value diversity in all its manifestations, but we're also potentially going to miss out on a ton of innovation that others who are different from us could have helped us generate.

Dolly Daydream

My niece Jennifer has a challenge that she shares with a number of people: dyslexia. She was teased at school and given labels like "dolly daydream" during her early years. It's understandable due to the fact that since she was a baby, she has had a habit of staring into space for long periods. She would hold her wide-eyed gaze into a seemingly distant universe, even when we would click our fingers in front of her face to try to get her attention.

"She's off with the fairies," people would remark, not realising how subtly demeaning this was for a young girl. This was the same "space cadet" who after years of encouragement and support from her parents and a selection of compatible schools, for her third-year interior architecture project created such a fresh and innovative interior design for a Swiss furniture company that she was given an industry award and flown out to Switzerland to collect it - as well as receiving a first-class honours for the project.

She actually helped design this book...

It was Sun Tzu who said, in the Art of War[3], long before neuroscience came along:

> *There are not more than five primary colours (blue, yellow, red, white, and black), yet in combination they produce more hues than can ever been seen*

So, if we're going to consider using colour as any kind of basis for describing differences, then we might use it to look at the variations in how we communicate. Let's look at some preferences in how we work, for example. Some of us will prefer to go about our business in a covert, deliberate and planned way in how we deal with other people in the workplace; some of us much prefer to let it all hang out, to share our moods and feelings in a much more transparent and open, spontaneous way. Let's call these two diverse colours red versus white, using Sun Tzu's system. And of course, there will be many hues in between the two extremes that cover all of us at varying times and in different moods as well. It's impossible to fix a person into a single, permanent label.

We can also experience variations in how we address one another. Some of us may value being quite direct, forceful, to the point, and even blunt, whereas others are much more comfortable being very circumspect, gentle, and diplomatic – even avoiding conflict if they possibly can. Let's call these blue versus yellow.

So, if we look at the subtle preferences we have in each of these two dimensions, and the hues in between, we can see that people naturally fall into a huge spectrum of varying colours, with variations in hue, tone, and saturation depending on our life journey, mood, and the situations we find ourselves in. And in our differences lie great potential for conflict. I enjoy sharing anecdotes about my experiences, for example, and I hate it when some people try to hurry me along or look away. I do admit, I can be a little overbearing sometimes, according to some, whereas others really enjoy this aspect of me. At least that's what they tell me!

My former boss Susanna

I had a manager once who was an Austrian lady. She was super-dynamic, positive, and results-driven. When I would report to her on my projects, I would enjoy sharing stories in some detail. She would soon become impatient and start tapping her fingers or a pen on the desk. She would even start completing my sentences for me! I was clearly mismatching her and not recognising how busy she was and under pressure to move on to the next priority she had. (I was dis-pacing her – see pacing in the next section.)

When I realised where I was going wrong, I soon learnt to prepare in advance a brief list of key details about my projects and to run through it quickly when we met. Making these changes transformed our relationship. We're still in touch today, 20 years on. And when we meet up occasionally, she even wants to hear some of my stories!

We need to fully appreciate and value all our differences – sex, race, religion, unique neural wiring, disabilities – both visible and invisible. Trying to achieve this challenges us all to create cultures of deep, positive allyship across our organisations. We must do this if we're to bring out and harness the full range of talents available in the human race to power up organisational performance. We also need to develop the systems and structures that support real inclusion.

85

Building rapport with people to inspire collaborative effort

Rapport is harmony, resonance, a feeling of being on the same wavelength as others. When we have rapport with people, we often feel on the same level as them. We open up, we move towards intimacy, trust develops.

Rapport is established and maintained with people we meet by pacing. By definition, this is the process of moving as the other person moves. It's about going with someone, rather than against them. Pacing or matching shows acceptance of the other person's behaviour and seeks to meet them in their model of the world. Have you ever found yourself naturally adjusting to someone you are 'in rapport' with? We sit in a similar position, talk about subjects we have in common, show empathy for how the other feels about things, we may even copy their manner and way of speaking and accent?

As we look to create positive, supportive relationships, we need to look at developing our skills in pacing others to build rapport.

Being able to connect with people of almost infinite variation requires:

1. Adopting an attitude of non-judgemental positive enquiry to experience another's experience and talent, in all its forms. In Stephen Covey's words, this is to "seek to understand before being understood."

2. Adapting our own natural style, views, opinions, tastes etc - to seek common ground with the other. We focus mindfully on our similarities, and delight in our differences.

The whole idea of a stereotype is to simplify. Instead of going through the problem of all this great diversity – that it's this or maybe that – you have just one large statement; it is this

Chinua Achebe

My personal eco-system

Once we are skilled at connecting with different people, we need to look at who we have, and who we need to weave into our world of inter-dependence. Who is in our molecule, who do we need to add, and how can we create positive, collaborative relationships with each person?

Using a map like the one featured here, you can make a note of the key people and use the different kinds of lines mentioned to symbolise your relationship with that person or group. You can use a big piece of paper and sticky notes to move things around. You can do this exercise with other people too.

Stakeholder mapping

Here is an example of a typical stakeholder map. Once you have identified the key people on whom your success depends, you can assess the quality of interaction you have with key people and teams.

Distance from you can represent how much impact they can have on you. Arrows can be used to represent the nature of the current relationship, e.g. who supports whom, supportive both ways, or just aware of each other's existence. Solid lines can indicate the strength of the relationship.

If you use physical sticky shapes you can stick one or flipcharts on a wall and work on the map with other people. Then you can explore how you want these relationships to develop by moving things around and adding notes. Your goal is to turn key relationships into mutually supportive and positive partnerships. This approach can work equally well at work and at home. There are online system such as Miro that can help if you want to do this exercise online.

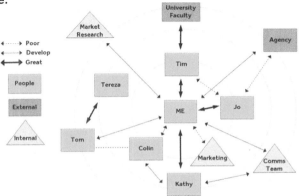

My positive role models

A good way to develop new practices is to observe others in action. You can look out for people who seem to create the right impact on other people - people who inspire respect and co-operation from the people they deal with.

Tony

I remember a senor vice president at American Express named Tony. He was my manager's manager's manager but he always showed an interest in the project I was working on - helping design a new IT system for HR. It was my first proper job in a commercial organisation. He would spot if I was looking challenged and would offer me a meeting. I would gladly accept as his meetings were always very positive and helpful. When I arrived for the meeting, he would get up from his desk, come to the door, welcome me into his office, close the door behind him, and sit with me.

He would fix his gaze on me, totally focusing on me, and ask me how things were going. I found it easy to share any issues and challenges as he was such a deep listener. I felt as if at that moment, me and my project were the only things he was interested in. Other managers I knew hardly looked up when I came into their workspace; they'd take a call, look at their computer screens while I was talking, or worse still, try to hurry me along with my input.

Tony was gently affirming in all he said and did. He would ask me questions:

What did you think is the blockage with this person or team? How else might we engage with them on this, do you think, Nick? What is the real result we want to achieve here?

He had a superb way of getting me to think through the challenge and to find my own solutions. He also never judged me. He behaved towards me as if I was a highly professional and capable person, all the time. He did offer some help, of course. Whether it was a message to another team asking for their help on this or popping into a meeting I would arrange to support me. He was the real deal and I would walk through walls for Tony.

He was a role model for me.

EXERCISE
WHO ARE MY ROLE MODELS?

List the names of four people whom you admire and who make the kind of impact you would like to make. These can be people you know well or people you have only seen from time to time.

1. Name: _____

How they influence me/others:

_____

_____

2. Name: _____

How they influence me/others:

_____

_____

3. Name: _____

How they influence me/others:

_____

_____

4. Name: _____

How they influence me/others:

_____

_____

Growing my eco-system

You are looking to cultivate relationships of trust and reciprocity.

- Learn about the teams and functions in your organisation and industry, and learn about external resources you might need (partners, customers, suppliers, competitors).

- Find ways to make contact. When you do, keep showing an interest in their world and in their challenges. Build rapport by pacing people.

- Include people with diverse talents and perspectives.

- Keep taking steps to nurture these connections with helpful updates of information and/or introductions to other people.

Harvesting my eco-system

- Specify what you need from someone and how to ask for it.

- Show respect for other peoples' time.

- Deal with conflict on a positive, conversational, respectful basis.

- Encourage a sense of community among members of the network.

- Bring people with diverse viewpoints into contact with each other.

- Highlight others' accomplishments and progress towards goals.

- Facilitate knowledge sharing across your network.

Sustaining my eco-system

- Keep adding new relationships and maintain those that have added value in the past.

- Expand your eco-system by contributing knowledge and helping others achieve success.

- Build your reputation by being reliable, trustworthy, and personable. If you can't meet someone's expectations, let them know asap.

90

Developing a collaborative eco-system

Much research has been done to look at how teams collaborate effectively. The Wilder Collaboration Factors[4] can help you highlight some ways to develop with a thorough review. Here are a few ideas...

Ten ways to improve collaboration in and between teams:

1. Build rapport, respect, understanding, and trust. **How will you create greater intimacy and support in your dealings?**

2. Be willing to help people get what they want. **What's in it for the other person/team to collaborate with you?**

3. Establish a shared vision and a sense of unique purpose. **How will you unite people behind a purpose that delivers real value for people?**

4. Get people into the habit of collaborating. **How can you establish a pattern of collaboration, perhaps even starting with smaller things?**

5. Make compromises. **When, where do you need to make them? Who may have conflicting interests? How can you create a 'win' for everyone?**

6. Widen participation. **How can you involve other people in inputting to key decisions about how things will be done?**

7. Measure success. **How can you get everyone working to the same measures of success? What feedback and encouragement can you give?**

8. Have a clear structure. **How can you ensure everyone knows their role? What is your process for decision-making and reviewing progress?**

9. Keep the water flowing. **How can you keep stimulating open dialogue between people? Be someone who asks good questions.**

10. Ensure sufficient resources. **Make sure there are the funds, materials, people, and time needed to achieve success. Act as a servant to the performance – be the enabler.**

We all need meaning in our lives to be happy. We need to feel trusted with some responsibility and competent in our ability. This book is designed to help you find more meaning in what you do. You can also help others achieve the same. If you can help people feel part of the creation of something of real value, it can help unite and motivate them.

The three bricklayers

There were once three bricklayers. There had been a great fire in 1666 that destroyed most of London. One of the world's most famous architects was working in the rebuilding of St Paul's Cathedral.

One day, he observed three bricklayers working on the rebuild. One was crouched down on his haunches working away but looking tired and half-hearted. Another was standing and working away looking just OK, but steady. The third was very engaged, working hard and fast, with great energy and enthusiasm. When he saw Wren watching him, he smiled back.

Wren asked the first bricklayer, "What are you working on?" to which the bricklayer replied, "What does it look like? I'm working away laying bricks to feed my family." The second bricklayer, responded, "I'm building a wall." But the third brick layer, when asked the question, "What are you doing?" replied with a gleam in his eye, "I'm a cathedral builder. I'm building a great cathedral that will be an inspiring place for hundreds of years to come."

Speaking up

There are times in life where we need to be able to make ourselves heard, where we aspire to have a deeper impact on how the organisation is functioning.

Becoming an influencer - thought leader

To get results in the modern organisation, we need to be able to assertively influence people who we may have little or no authority over. For some important issues we may need to speak persuasively upwards in the context of the organisation structure. There are two categories of these people we want to influence:

- People we have equal standing with in the organisation: team members and peers.
- People who have higher standing in the organisation: senior leaders and key figures.

I have potential to be an influencer-thought leader in these areas:

1._____

2._____

3._____

The world around us is evolving at breakneck speed. People are experiencing exponentially higher volumes of content and getting on the radar of people we want to influence effectively is a tough challenge.

We must be someone who communicates important priorities persuasively and authentically with key internal and external audiences: in meetings, through our emails, at forums, events, panel discussions, conferences - inside and outside the organisation, both virtually and face-to-face.

There are many meetings where a mediocre, plainly self-serving or an under-prepared communicator can mean a lost opportunity for themselves to gain influence, and at worst can cause permanent damage to their reputation.

Many communicators so easily fall into bad habits with presentations (especially with the advent of online presentations). They retreat to a comfort zone, repeating content or reading out the same spiel blindly recycling pre-canned slides and ultimately fail to connect in any meaningful way.

To build up your status as an Influencer-Thought Leader in your areas of expertise requires:

- A strong eco-system made up of key stakeholders
- A clear personal value proposition
- Communication plan: what/when to share
- Strong delivery skills: how to best share it

We need to keep things growing through our clear intention to make regular investments in actions to enhance your perceived value and connection with key people throughout your eco-system.

My personal value proposition

Your personal value proposition should clearly identify the benefits that you can bring to the key people you want to influence in your organisation, and it needs to be relevant and resonant with their most important challenges and priorities – what keeps them awake at night:

Key Stakeholders	What keeps them awake at night	Benefits I can offer	How/when to share these

Actions for me:

_____

_____

_____

_____

_____

_____

_____

_____

Be water, my friend.
Empty your mind.
Be formless, shapeless, like water.
You put water into a cup, it becomes the cup.
You put water into a bottle, it becomes the bottle.
You put it into a teapot, it becomes the teapot.
Now water can flow, or it can crash.
Be water, my friend.

Bruce Lee

PRINCIPLE 6
References and further reading

[1] Mike Pegg: https://www.thepositiveencourager.global/
[2] Sir Ken Robinson tells the story of Gillian Lynne; "Do schools kill creativity?": You Tube
[3] The Art of War; Sun Tzu; Pax Librorum; 2009
[4] Wilder Collaboration Factors: www.brauchtworks.com/yahoo_site_admin/assets/docs/Wilder_Collaboration_Factors_Inventory_and_Interpretation_Guide_180218.48132945.pdf

For any thoughts or feelings...

_____

_____

_____

_____

_____

_____

_____

_____

_____

_____

_____

_____

_____

PRINCIPLE 7
CREATE VALUE FOR PEOPLE

What is the good fruit I can create in this world?

Do you wonder how some people are able to accomplish so much? What makes some people so productive in life? And what do we mean by productive?

For our Shallow Self, the idea of fruit is all about what we can secure and consume for ouselves, ideally without having to do too much to get it. One could argue that our climate crisis is a symptom of the triumph of the self-centred human ego over the instincts of what our deeper moral compass tells us. While people take more than they give back then this eco-system we depend on will surely keep on deteriorating.

The Net Positive Life

When you look back to your example of your Best Self in action, who benefitted from what you did? What value did you create for others? Were the benefits you created more than the resources you used? This is the idea of Net Positive in essence: creating more than we take.

The Greeks had four words for different types of love:

Storge: Natural affection for others
Eros: Sexual desire for another
Philia: Deeper, more emotional affection or friendship with others
Agape: Unconditional giving, making personal sacrifices for others

Of course, it's Agape where our Deeper Self created true Net Positives and paradoxically gives us real meaning in life, one of the main factors in being happy and content with life. Whether it's creating high value experiences for customers, contributing to a great team effort, doing community work, helping a friend through a crisis, helping clean up the environment.

The simple rule is: the more value we create, the more we receive.

The Goose That Laid Golden Eggs (Aesop)

This is a quite well known story about a man and his wife who buy a baby goose. They feed it and nurture it and one day it lays an egg. It's no ordinary egg. It is a golden egg. They take the egg to town and are offered a good sum of money for it.

As they get richer by selling the eggs, they become greedy for more. One egg a day is just not providing all the money they need to buy all the lovely things they want. They start to become restless and dissatisfied. The husband and wife start arguing over the slightest thing as they become frustrated at not being able to get more gold from the goose.

They think they are not getting rich fast enough, so they imagine the goose's stomach must be made of gold. So, one day, they decide to cut it open. But they are dissappointed to find...there is no gold inside.

In the end, they lose the gifts they were given by wanting more without giving back. Their greed leads them to destroy the very source of all that's good in their lives. They end up swimming around in the mud blaming everyone else but not themselves and most of all their greedy egos.

Be courageous

I am brave

It takes courage to create value for others and live a Net Positive life:

Body: Resilient, aware, fit and proactive
Mind: Learning, unlearning and relearning, openly and flexibly
Heart: Experiencing emotions fully (good & bad) but not getting stuck
Soul: Living with purpose and acting with agape

This book has been about learning how to live a life of non-frantic peace and power. It's about how through simplicity and serenity we can bear so much more fruit than we consume.

Applying these principles may not guarantee you more years in your life but they will give you more life in the years you do have.

Everytime we draw in the next breath, the water we drink, the food we eat, we create the capacity to build on our strengths and create value for all the people in our lives. We must take care of the goose...

98

The principle of reciprocity

One of the key principles the farmer and his wife failed to grasp was that we get out of life what we put in. If we consume fruit without helping develop the conditions for trees to flourish, we are simply depleting the system that support us. Worse still is when we seek pleasure in ways that deplete us: body, mind, heart and soul.

When we allow our Shallow Self to run the show, we just seek maximum reward for ourselves at all times. Our tree will soon begin to show signs of ill health and the quality of the 'fruit' we produce will reflect this: the experiences we create for customers and colleagues; how good a friend, partner, or parent we are; our character; our contribution to others' lives; and ultimately, how we see our lives as we approach the end of them. This is the real gold we will be counting near the end and what we will be remembered for when we move on...

The Deeper Self is capable of working in a different way, a richer and more satisfying way. When we create fruit at this level, we experience feelings of love, joy, peace, patience, self-control...and we can be known by the people we most care about for our kindness, goodness, faithfulness, tenderness, and gentleness.

Of course, this kind of gold is not what the ego-mind is seeking: a bigger house, a better paid job, a new car, a lovely holiday, awards, status, recognition. Of course, achieving these things as a result of creating fruit in our lives is a great experience and a measure of our success. These things can be evidence of our achievements.

The trouble starts when the way we achieve these things has not created any lasting value for anyone - when we have no gold at the end, and all we're doing is either killing the goose or farming them until they die of disease and misery.

Australian nurse Bronnie Ware* spent many years working in palliative care, taking care of patients who knew they only had weeks left to live. In her book 'Regrets of the Dying', Bronnie talks about the five most common regrets people have.

My own experience with both of my parents who both passed away far too early bears out Bronnie's findings.

(*https://bronnieware.com/blog/regrets-of-the-dying/)

A good life well lived?

As we begin to run out of the time we have in this life, we may spend time looking in the rear view mirror at how we lived our life.

According to Bronnie. one of the most common things people say at the end of their lives is:

I wish I'd let myself be happier

To live a good life, we need to look in the mirror today to see what make changes we need to make now, not wait until it's all in the rear view. Are you happy with how you are living your life today? Are you doing OK enough in terms of money, property, and/or prestige but still feeling empty? Are you experiencing happiness, love, joy and peace at work and home? Are you making yourself and other people happy through your kindness, goodness, and loyalty? Are you experiencing the fruits that come through applying the principles we've covered? What matters most in your life? How can you create and attract more of these things in your life?

In essence, this book is about living a good life from your Deeper Self rather than letting the reactive Shallow Self run the show. It's about being rooted in your purpose and values. It's about being the conductor of your life, not just a puppet being operated by others' demands, societal expectations and your own knee jerk reactions. It's about the pursuit of wisdom and understanding to avoid the mistakes that can cause pain for ourselves and others.

What are the experiences you want to have in the future? What are the things you want to or need to learn? What fruits do you want to produce for yourself and others in this world? Only you can decide what you want your life to mean.

We've talked about making sure you spend time in the good soil and reduce the time in the bad soil. How can you best look after your physical, mental, emotional, and spiritual wellbeing? What daily and weekly practices do you want to implement to help create a good tree that bears good fruit? How can you work and live in a positive, balanced, structured, calm, and controlled way, not simply reacting from moment to moment?

We've also talked about the value of water and the need to cultivate quality relationships with others where we feel we can communicate authentically. This is the living water we need to share with others so that we can be our best selves and grow together happily. How can you be who you really are with yourself and other people?

We might have hundreds of Facebook friends, be on and off WhatsApp every day, connect with people, and comment on their Instagram posts... but how many of these people do we really know? Are we connecting meaningfully with the real person when we communicate at work or home, when a young person wants to play with us, or tell us a story from their world? Who are the important people you want to keep in touch with?

I hope that this book has helped you clarify some of the fruits you want to create in your life. Much of the content has been the result of some mistakes I had to learn from.

I hope you will seek the gold, and drop the mould.

This entire book has been inspired by a description in an ancient text of what it is to be a person who lives a virtuous, high quality life:

Be like a tree
Planted by rivers of water
Bearing fruit in my season
My leaf will not wither
And everything I do will prosper.
...not be like chaff that the wind just blows away...

Before we sign-off, how about making five commitments to yourself, to others and the world we live in, to become:

The Mindful Communicator

101

MY COMMITMENTS TO ME, OTHERS, THE WORLD

How will you use your capabilities to produce good fruits in this life?

I want to:

1. _____

_____

2. _____

_____

3. _____

_____

4. _____

_____

5. _____

_____

Make sure you add images and some of these words to your vision board.

Wishing you and your loved ones every blessing and a life well lived, full of good fruit.

Nicholas Brice
The Business Soulman.

SOME ADDITIONAL IDEAS

PRINCIPLE 1
Be fully present

Some quotes about being fully present:

This is a transcription of a speech by Eckhart Tolle published by Aby Vohra in The Courage to Awaken.

Anything that you could obtain in life on a personal level, whatever you manifest, is the icing on the cake – because you already have the cake. You are the cake! (laughing) If you don't realize that, then life is frustrating because whatever you manifest, if you think that's the cake, it's not going to satisfy you for long. It might even make you sick if you eat too much cake (laughing). The true, healthful cake is the essence of who you are – intense, alive presence. That's the fullness of life.

You can only be successful at manifesting if you don't need whatever it is that you want to manifest in order to give you the experience of 'having made it', a fuller sense of identity. You may want to have a better place to live. But you don't need it to experience the fullness of life.

People don't want the thing that they think they want, they want the feeling which that thing will give them. You don't want the car just for the sake of the car, you want the feeling that is associated with the car. The car itself is meaningless. People want this fullness of life through something else.

You are already the fullness of life itself, the unconditioned consciousness. Jesus said, 'Find the kingdom of heaven within you, and all the things that you think you need will be added onto you.'

Ultimately, you are not dependent on external conditions. You are not at the mercy of what's happening or not happening around you. This is a wonderful realization, a wonderful freedom.

Time spent among trees is never time wasted.
Anonymous

Meditation can strengthen the immune system, lower stress, reduce anxiety, calm the heart rate, and reduce blood pressure.
Doctor's Health Press

PRINCIPLE 2
Know who you are

Some quotes about solitude and discovering who you really are:

Solitude is dangerous. It's very addictive. It becomes a habit after you realize how calm and peaceful it is. It's like you don't want to deal with people anymore because they drain your energy.
Jim Carrey

Which is worth more, a crowd of thousands, or your own genuine solitude? Freedom, or power over an entire nation? A little while alone in your room will prove more valuable than anything else that could ever be given you.
Rumi

It's beautiful to be alone. To be alone does not mean to be lonely. It means the mind is not influenced or contaminated by society.
Jiddu Krishnamurti

If you cannot be at ease with yourself when alone, you will seek a relationship to cover up your unease. You can be sure that the unease will then reappear in some other form within the relationship, and you will probably hold your partner responsible for it.
Eckhart Tolle

Be a loner. That gives you time to wonder, to search for the truth. Have holy curiosity. Make your life worth living.
Albert Einstein

Ordinary men hate solitude.
But the Master makes use of it,
embracing his aloneness, realizing
he is one with the whole universe.
Lao Tzu

Be alone, that is the secret of invention;
be alone, that is when ideas are born.
Nikola Tesla

You are not alone as a person,
you are alone as the entire universe.
Mooji

PRINCIPLE 3
Create the conditions

Some quotes about creating the right conditions:

The Earth is what we all have in common.
Wendell Berry

Every human being has both sets of forces within him. One set clings to safety and defensiveness out of fear, tending to regress backward, hanging on to the past, afraid to grow away from the primitive communication with the mother's uterus and breast, afraid to take chances, afraid to jeopardize what he already has, afraid of independence, freedom and separateness. The other set of forces impels him forward toward wholeness of Self and uniqueness of Self, toward full functioning of all his capacities, toward confidence in the face of the external world at the same time that he can accept his deepest, real, unconscious Self.
Abraham H. Maslow (Toward a Psychology of Being)

Connecting with others gives us a sense of inclusion, connection, interaction, safety, and community. Your vibe attracts your tribe, so if you want to attract positive and healthy relationships, be one! Staying connected and getting reconnected feeds the flow of goodness which empowers our humanity.
Susan C. Young

In the units that lacked psychological safety, health care professionals hid their errors, fearing retribution. As a result, they weren't able to learn from their mistakes. In the units with high psychological safety, on the other hand, reporting errors made it possible to prevent them...
Adam M. Grant (Give and Take: A Revolutionary Approach to Success[1])

Convince yourself everyday that you are worthy of a good life. Let go of stress, breathe. Stay positive, all is well.
Germany Ken

Norway has 5.4 million people, yet dominated the 2022 Winter Olympics.
Our system is not set up for success. It's more a system for joy and happiness, to have joy with your sport and be healthy. And maybe that's why we are successful. We aim to really enjoy what we do.
Vetle Christiansen, who won gold in the team biathlon

[1] Give and Take: A Revolutionary Approach to Success; Adam M.Grant; W&N (2013)

PRINCIPLE 4
Be intentional

Some quotes about being intentional:

Our words have power. They impact others, but they also impact us.
Michael Hyatt

Intentional living is the art of making our own choices before others' choices make us.
Richie Norton

When your intentions are pure, so too will be your success.
Charles Glassman MD

It's not enough to have lived. We should be determined to live for something.
Winston Churchil

Many people would like eternal life... without even knowing how to spend the next weekend.
Claus Moller

We are a culture that confuses busyness with purpose. Social media with connection. Instagram scrolling with therapy and spiritual direction. Wealth with wellbeing. And self-obsession with vulnerability.
Karen Joy Hardwick, The Connected Leader: 7 Strategies to Empower Your True Self and Inspire Others

When we have to do something we don't like doing or want to do, we can either say 'No', or volunteer to do them by choice by saying: 'YES, I will do this!' - and doing it well. We might even find some gold in the experience.
Nicholas Brice, The Business Soulman

For you to be able to thrive in the workplace, you have to be intentional about how you spend your time. Anything you leave to chance, or are not committed to, will eventually fall apart. If you are a parent, you have to be intentional with the time you spend with your kids; if you are married, you have to be intentional with the time you spend with your spouse, if you want to be physically fit, you have to be intentional about it.
Evi Idoghor

PRINCIPLE 5
Organise your thoughts & communications

Some quotes about being organised in thought and speech:

You cannot eat an elephant in one mouthful. But you will succeed if you take one mouthful at a time.
Claus Moller

You can have anything you want, but not everything. If it was really important to spend an afternoon at my daughter's school, I had to think, how was I going to organize my life to do that? How could I become more efficient? I always tried to put my priorities on the table, personal and professional, and work around them.
Laura Lang

Whether you're a newspaper journalist, a lawyer, a doctor, you have to organize your thoughts.
Frederick Wiseman

Literal cleanliness and orderliness can release us from abstract cognitive and affective distress - just consider how, during moments where life seems to be spiraling out of control, it can be calming to organize your clothes, clean the living room, get the car washed.
Robert Sapolsky

Mostly I make lists for projects. This can be daunting. Breaking something big into its constituent parts will help you organize your thoughts, but it can also force you to confront the depth of your ignorance and the hugeness of the task. That's OK. The project may be the lion, but the list is your whip.
Adam Savage

A successful presentation needs to be both buttoned up (orderly) and free-flowing (a conversation). The tension between the two, the fact that both things are happening at once, defines the process.
Dale Ludwig and Greg Owen-Boger

New research into cognitive functioning - how the brain works - proves that bullet points are the least effective way to deliver important information. Neuroscientists are finding that what passes as a typical presentation is usually the worst way to engage your audience.
Carmine Gallo, The Presentation Secrets of Steve Jobs

PRINCIPLE 6
Cultivate mindful interactions

Some quotes about cultivating mindful interactions:

Because of the internet and communications, the clash of cultures is much more direct. People feel, I think, less certain about their identity, less certain about economic security.
Barack Obama

You only ever have three things: 1) your self, wellbeing and mindset 2) Your life network, resources and resourcefulness 3) Your reputation and goodwill. Treasure and tend the first. Value, support and build the second. And mindfully, wisely ensure that the third (your life current and savings account) is always in credit.
Rasheed Ogunlaru

Be bold! Step out of your comfort zone, burn down the stereotypes, the labels, the categories, and build a community.
Kaylee Stepkoski

When we get too caught up in the busyness of the world, we lose connection with one another – and ourselves.
Jack Kornfield

Indifference and neglect often do much more damage than outright dislike.
J.K. Rowling, Harry Potter and the Order of the Phoenix

We often add to our pain and suffering by being overly sensitive, over-reacting to minor things and sometimes taking things too personally.
The Dalai Lama

Never look down on anybody unless you're helping them up.
Jesse Jackson

You have to accept that some people are never going to be for you. Treat them with respect, but you don't need their approval to fulfill your destiny.
Joel Osteen

Most people do not listen with the intent to understand; they listen with the intent to reply.
Stephen R. Covey

108

PRINCIPLE 7
Create value for people

Some quotes about creating value for people:

The Meraki moment. This is a word that originated in Greece.
It is when you commit yourself fully to something: heart and soul.

The concept of idolatory seems to include the idea that something external/material can fulfil us internally. When we drink life through the heart and soul and produce fruit - real value - we often feel a deeper joy: giving unconditionally, spending time in nature, investing in human connection. Sure, we can create material wealth, and that's great fun too of course, but what truly quenches the thirst are things we can't often see.
Nicholas Brice, The Business Soulman.

Anchor the eternity of love in your own soul and embed this planet with goodness. Lean toward the whispers of your own heart, discover the universal truth, and follow its dictates. Release the need to hate, to harbor division, and the enticement of revenge. Release all bitterness. Hold only love, only peace in your heart, knowing that the battle of good to overcome evil is already won. Choose confrontation wisely, but when it is your time don't be afraid to stand up, speak up, and speak out against injustice. And if you follow your truth down the road to peace and the affirmation of love, if you shine like a beacon for all to see, then the poetry of all the great dreamers and philosophers is yours to manifest in a nation, a world community, and a Beloved Community that is finally at peace with itself.
John Lewis
John Lewis (1940 - 2020) began his life preaching to chickens at his parents' farm in Alabama and rose to the House of Representatives in 1988, being reelected 18 times. He participated in the 1960 Nashville sit-ins, the Freedom Rides, was the chairman of the Student Nonviolent Coordinating Committee (SNCC) from 1963 to 1966, and was one of the "Big Six" leaders of groups who organized the 1963 March on Washington. He fulfilled many key roles in the civil rights movement throughout his life.

You can have what you want if you help other people get what they want.
Zig Ziglar

I've been a so-called coward and a so-called hero and there's not the thickness of a sheet of paper between them. Maybe cowards and heroes are just ordinary men who, for a split second, do something out of the ordinary. That's all. It's not what you do, it's why you do it. That's the eye of the needle.
Lord Jim, Joseph Conrad

ABOUT THE AUTHOR

Nicholas Brice is an international speaker-host-coach, performance consultant and theatre producer/director of the award-winning Edinburgh sellout show: The Big Bite-Size Breakfast Show. He is co-author of Brand Alchemy (Blackhall Publishing; 2007) - a book about building brands through people.

In his early managerial career in the 1980's with American Express he worked alongside Time Manager International on the culture transformations that helped SAS and British Airways achieve industry leading performance and profitability. Helping achieve similar outcomes for American Express Nicholas went on to work at the forefront of a range of leading national and international customer experience culture change projects with TMI and his own business, Visions. He has helped some of the world's leading businesses in motor retail, food and fashion retail, financial services, airlines, public-private sector transitions, local council, airlines, distribution, manufacturing, telecoms, professional services, insurance. Clients include Unipart, Toyota-Lexus Europe, USA and Japan, Kerzner International, BSkyB, British Airways, Sony, Mercedes, Equant (Orange), Lucent and Progress.

Most recently he helped develop and embed the performance ethos at the new American Express Community Stadium, home of Brighton's Football Club, and the new Tottenham Hotspur Stadium, with both projects winning major international awards.

Nicholas was at the heart of the team that originated the concept of Moments of Truth and the practices of Customer Journey Mapping and Culture Audits as they evolved into the benchmark methods they are today.

Nicholas is a thoughtful, inventive, flexible and excellent facilitator. His sessions are bright, fun and engaging and his presentation skills are very charismatic.
James Hunt, Director of Entertainment, Production and Sky Arts HD, BSkyB.

His approachable and easy going-manner coupled with his insider industry knowledge and service expertise proved a real hit with our delegates. They are known for being a tough bunch - he was able to train and coach them and at times deliver difficult messages using a unique style of anecdote and humour.
Anthony Coombes, Head of Training, British Airways and LOCOG.

Nicholas spearheaded our transformation to an international multi-award winning venue. His tools and methods have been a pivotal ingredient in our success.
Rose Read, Head of People and Culture, Brighton & Hove Albion FC.

Wth his company, Soul Corporations®, he has won National Training Journal Gold awards for Change Management, Leadership Development, Learning Partnership; Engage Business Media award for Best Customer and Employee Engagement Programme. At the time of writing (Sept 2022) we are finalists with Progress in the USA for the Engage Awards for Best Customer and Employee Engagement Programme, Best Internal Communications Programme and Best Use of Training.

The Soul Corporations® holos is a symbol of the whole person acting in harmony with themselves, with each other and with the environment. The seven colours represent seven chakras. In Ayurveda and various yoga traditions, such as Tantra and Kundalini, the term chakra refers to an energy centre that interacts with both the physical and energetic bodies. The interconnectedness of the system conveys the idea of interdependency, balance and harmony, in body, mind, heart and soul.

www.soulcorporations.com

NICHOLAS BRICE
THE BUSINESS SOULMAN

www.nicholasbrice.com

Printed in Great Britain
by Amazon

86816383R00066